BJ
1249
.D851...   liberation

ETHICS AND THE THEOLOGY OF LIBERATION

Ethics and the Theology of Liberation

Enrique Dussel

Translated by Bernard F. McWilliams, C.SS.R.

Maryknoll, New York 10545

The Catholic Foreign Mission Society of America (Maryknoll) recruits and trains people for overseas missionary service. Through Orbis Books Maryknoll aims to foster the international dialogue which is essential to mission. The books published, however, reflect the opinions of their authors and are not meant to represent the official position of the Society.

Originally published as *Teología de la liberación y ética, Caminos de liberación latinoamericana II*, copyright © 1974 by Latinoamerica Libros SRL, Junín 969, Buenos Aires, Argentina

English translation copyright © 1978 by Orbis Books, Maryknoll, NY 10545

All rights reserved

Printed in the United States of America

Library of Congress Cataloging in Publication Data

Dussel, Enrique D
   Ethics and the theology of liberation.

   Translation of Teología de la liberación y ética.
   Originally delivered as lectures at a course organized by the Justice and Peace Study Center, Buenos Aires, 1972.
   1. Christian ethics—Catholic authors—Addresses, essays, lectures. 2. Church—Addresses, essays, lectures. 3. Woman (Christian theology)—Addresses, essays, lectures. 4. Knowledge, Theory of—Addresses, essays, lectures. 5. Liberation theology—Addresses, essays, lectures. I. Title.
BJ1249.D8513   241'.04'2   77-13397
ISBN 0-88344-115-2
ISBN 0-88344-116-0 pbk.

They [the temple authorities of Israel]
began their accusation by saying:
"We found this man [Jesus]
inciting our people to revolt. . . .

He [Pilate] then said to them:
"You brought this man before me . . .
as a *political agitator.*"

Pilate then gave his verdict:
Their demand was to be granted.

And though Herod [Hebrew puppet ruler]
and Pilate [surrogate of the Roman emperor]
had been enemies before,
they were reconciled that same day.

Luke 23:1, 4, 14, 24, 12–13; emphasis added

Lord, forgive me for getting used to seeing children
who seem to be eight years old
and are really thirteen.
Lord, forgive me for getting used to
sloshing around in the mud.
I can leave, they can't.
Lord, forgive me for learning
to put up with contaminated water.
I can get away from it, they can't.
Lord, forgive me whenever I switch on the light
and forget that they can't.
Lord, I can go on a hunger strike but not they;
how can the hungry go on a hunger strike?
Lord, forgive me for telling them
that "not by bread alone does man live"
and not fighting all out for their bread.
Lord, I want to love them for them,
and not for me. Help me.
Lord, I dream of dying for them:
Help me to live for them.
Lord, I want to be with them when the light comes.
Help me.

> Prayer of Carlos Mugica (d. May 11, 1974), member of the Movement of Priests for the Third World in Argentina, liberation martyr, incorruptible prophet of the dispossessed, murdered by those who fear to face a people free from oppression

CONTENTS

Preface   xi

1. *Theologal Anthropology I: Ethics as Destructive Criticism*   1
   Fifteenth-Century Ecumenes and the Origin
      of Dependency   2
   Totality as Flesh or "My World"   4
   European Expansion   8
   The Prophets Against the Idol. The Atheism of Jesus   13
   Sin as a Totalization of the System   17
   The Sin of Adam   21
   Institutional Inheritance of the Sin of Theft   25

2. *Theologal Anthropology II: Ethics as Liberation
      Criticism*   28
   Dead Flesh: The Totalized System   29
   Incarnation as the "Death of Death"   31
   The Paschal Incarnation of Liberation   33
   The Three Meanings of "Poor"   36
   Toward a Christian Ethic of Liberation   38
   The Logic of Sin   41
   The Violence of Sin   43
   The Ethos of Liberation   46
   More About Violence   48
   "Being-in-the-Money"   49

3. *The Theology of Politics: Toward a Latin American
      Ecclesiology*   52
   Preliminary Clarifications   53
   The Erotic, Pedagogical, and Political Relationships   55
   Ecclesiology as Politics and Pedagogy   59
   Ecclesial Prehistory and Protohistory   60
   The First Cultural Totalization of Christianity   64
   First Thesis: The Church "Before" the World   66
   Second Thesis: The Church "in" the World   68
   Third Thesis: The Church as Prophetic Institution   72
   Prophetico-Pedagogical Function of the Church
      in the World   78
   Mystery as "Breaking Down the Barriers"   83

The Church, Liberating Force of History   87
The Sacraments (as Consecration and Celebration) and
    Ministries (as a Function) of Liberation   89

4. Alienation and Liberation of Woman in the Church:
    A Treatment of the Erotic in Theology   100
  Toward a History of the Erotic   101
  The Erotic in Latin America   105
  The Being of Woman and Her Alienation   108
  Feminism and Women's Liberation   110
  The Erotic in Christian Thinking. Liberation of the
    Consecrated Woman   112
  Miriam of Nazareth, Virgin of Guadalupe: A Free and Freeing
    Woman   117

5. The Situation of the Christian Thinker in Latin America:
    Epistemological Reflection on the Ontological Level   120
  The Meaning of Thinking   121
  Crisis as a Condition for Thinking   123
  Scholasticism and the Modern Period   130
  Beyond Scholasticism and Modernity:
    The Hermeneutic Question   132
  The Need for Creative, Historical, Concrete, Committed,
    Asystematic, Prophetic, Anguished Thought   141
  The Dangerous Situation of Thought   145

6. The Theology of Liberation: Epistemological Status   149
  Imitative and European Theology   149
  Modern Europeans: The "I" as Foundation   151
  Awareness, Faith, and Abstract Theoretical Theology   153
  Solipsism in Existential Theology   157
  Lack of Historico-Political Mediation in the "Theology of
    Hope"   159
  Lack of International Vision in Political Theology   162
  Peoples' Struggle Before Class Struggle   163
  Liberation Theology?   165
  Revelation of the Interpretative Categories   167
  Faith as Interpretation   170
  Theology as the "Analectic Pedagogy of Eschatological
    Liberation"   173

Preface

These chapters, which are a continuation of lectures published under the title *History and the Theology of Liberation* (Maryknoll, New York: Orbis Books, 1976), were originally delivered orally. They are part of a course I gave in Buenos Aires, Argentina, in November 1972. Two lectures that I gave on other occasions have been included in this book. I have developed the theme of this book more in detail in courses given at the Latin American Bishops' Pastoral Institute (Quito, Ecuador), at the Theological Institute of the Catholic University of Valparaiso (Chile), to the theological faculty of Louvain (Belgium), to groups of bishops (fifty-two in Medellín, Colombia, in 1971, twenty-seven in Guatemala in 1972), to provincials of religious orders in Medellín on two occasions, etc. In the manner in which the lectures appear here, they were given in a course entitled "Church and Liberation," organized by the Justice and Peace Study Center (Nazareth House, Buenos Aires). There a group of laypeople and priests met for three days to listen to and discuss the reflections that make up this book. The oral style has not been eliminated, and the occasional imprecise choice of word should be attributed to the spontaneity of the moment.

The two lectures I have added are on women's liberation (chapter 4), given in a course for CIDOC (Cuernavaca, Mexico) in 1973, and on the task of Latin American thinkers (chapter 5), given in San Miguel, Buenos Aires, in 1970. The latter deals with a problem that antedates liberation theology. I include it because it is a presage of what was to come within a few months.

In an excellent contribution on the theology of liberation Héctor Borrat spoke of the necessity of a "firm turn of the rudder" to get the people of God in exile back on a New Testament course (*Víspera,* no. 30, 1973). These lectures, given months before his remark, already *explicitly* had the intention of referring almost exclusively to the New Testament and even to the Apostles' Creed (quotations from which appear as epigraphs for most of the chapters of this book).

Second, Borrat points out that in this theology Christ has not come into his own. For my part, I had already determined to give a christological view of reality in these lectures. I was tempted to entitle one lecture "The Antichrist" or "Demonology," that is, the pre-Christian situation of sin under the reign of the "prince of this world." The second chapter in this volume is Christology pure and simple. The third is an "ecclesiology," as its title indicates, but considered from the christological standpoint as the theological moment of the Incarnation.

Third, we are reminded by Borrat of a serious omission in liberation theology—Mary. We have included consideration of her in the chapter on women's liberation but only to underscore what we would call "liberation Mariology," i.e., the Mariology of the Virgin of Guadalupe emblazoned on the banners of Hidalgo's armies or of the one who subversively proclaimed, "He has pulled down princes from their thrones and exalted the lowly."

The lectures have a certain order. In the first place, they deal with a theologal anthropology in its negative aspect. It was necessary to get down to first things, and the first things are ethical options. Ethics—the first kind of theology—is a fundamental theology. Whoever hopes to begin theology with a kind of "theory of theologal studies," is simply opting ethically for a certain course; all future thought will be traceable to an initial option that was never questioned or even thought about. What you then have is ideological theology. This is the topic we take up in the first and second lectures. We go from a demonology to a Christology.

Arriving at theologal fact and choosing to stay within the boundaries of revelation, we find ourselves from the beginning living in a community of faith, a prophetic institution. We thus go from ethics to theologal politics as pedagogical function. For this reason ethics is followed by an ecclesiology, a matter of extreme timeliness and urgency in Latin America.

As noted above, I have added two lectures to the original course—one on women's place in the church, a topic treating the erotic (chapter 4), the other on epistemology (chapter 5), as an introduction to the last lecture.

Finally, in the sixth chapter, I go deeply into the epistemological level of liberation theology, since some people in Europe and Latin America are opposed to this theological manner of thinking. I have wanted to continue the debate and, from certain aspects, even open the debate, so that the theology out of Latin America will grow along with the continent in its agony of liberation. At any rate, as a French thinker and friend said, "Against wind and tide there was born in Latin America a theology that was its own, the first theology not exported from Europe."

History and the Theology of Liberation (1976) was a *historico*-theological interpretation of Latin America. This series of lectures, by contrast, is an *ethico*-theological interpretation; I tend to stay on a somewhat more abstract level and I deal with categories that have already been outlined in their anthropological aspects in my work *Para una ética de la liberación latinoamericana* (Buenos Aires: Siglo XXI, 1973–74). My purpose has not been to attack new problems—even though there are new problems—but rather, to pull together the loose ends of liberation theology from an epistemological point of view. At any rate, we have so far only been stating the questions: We will have to wrestle with them for a long while before we have a well-built, lasting road.

1

Theologal Anthropology I: Ethics as Destructive Criticism

> *Our Father . . .*
> *save us from the Evil One.*
> Matt. 6: 9, 13

These first two chapters take up the matter of theologal anthropology, that is, a theological consideration of the being of the person. The first chapter enters into a consideration of the last phrase of the Lord's Prayer: "Save us from the Evil One" (Matt. 6:13). I prefer this translation to "deliver us from evil." The Evil One, of course, is the Devil. This will be a chapter mainly about the Evil One, the Devil, but viewed from the standpoint of Latin America.

What I say about Latin America is valid for what today we call the "periphery" (which includes Africa and Asia as well); a realistic look at world history will indicate this. Evil is by no means confined to the private sector, something I do all by myself. The "prince of this world" structures everything to his advantage. If right now I could pin a name on evil—a name in line with current history—I would call it "detente." Evil can also be a world power that we are a part of: a world order in which there seems to be a benign justice and things get done because there is peace under the security of law. One who would liberate us from the Evil One will thus have to start from something very concrete.

In the second chapter I shall be talking about the words "He died under Pontius Pilate," because the just person dies under the power of sin. This is the major theme of contemporary Latin American theology. Latin American theology does not start with existing theologies but with the real and concrete totality of what is taking place. Neither does it start with a relationship of the solitary self with another individual self but considers the structure in which the sin of the world conditions our own personal sin.

Fifteenth-Century Ecumenes and the Origin of Dependency

A little more than five hundred years ago, Bartolomé de las Casas was born in Seville. In that epoch Isabel de Castilla married Fernando de Aragón, thus achieving the unity of Spain. On our planet there were then seven great "ecumenes," that is to say, seven horizons of understanding, unique spheres of power outside of which were nothing but barbarians. Later we will see that the ecumene (as a totality) is a theological category.

The first ecumene is *Latin* Europe, the Europe that opposed the Arabs who from the east and from the south had, for eight centuries, impeded its expansion to the Orient. The second is the little that was left of the Byzantine world after its conquest by the Turks in 1453. The resplendent Christendom of the Orient practically disappeared in the fifteenth century.

Next there is the empire of the Hindu kingdoms,

where there is also a Buddhist presence that is mostly Brahmin. There is China, where Marco Polo in the thirteenth century viewed the natives as barbarians. Going across the Pacific, we come to the Mayan-Aztec world. We see it and the Incan world to the south as another "center of the universe." Every ecumene sees itself as the center of the universe. The Incas in Peru called their city Cuzco, a name meaning "navel of the world"; for the Jews the center of the world was Mount Zion. Every culture sees itself as containing the ultimate totality of meaning. It is the place where the gods communicate with human beings in the way that a mother communicates with her child through the umbilical cord. All these ecumenes were self-contained, "totalized" worlds and had practically no contact with other worlds. That is, until 1492. In that year, Europeans were able to go west across the Atlantic and achieve what they had never been able to do before, namely, slip out of the enclosure the Arab world had erected around them. When the Atlantic was conquered, the geopolitical organization of the world changed completely. The discovery of America by Spain and Portugal gave Europe elbow room for development and an end to their entrapment.

What would they now do about the Arabs? Simply surround them. The navigating of the Cape provided Europe with a water route to India. The ancient route through the Middle East, so long dominated by the Arabs, would now no longer be needed because the produce of China, Japan, and India could be brought home by sea. Thus the Arabs ceased to be the center of the world. The Mediterranean basin, which had been the geopolitical center of the world for almost five thousand years, gives way to the Atlantic. Now Europe can conquer the whole world, known and unknown, and it now occupies the center of the world. The rest becomes periphery. Thus was born a situation in the fifteenth century that has perdured until the twentieth; we call all this the colonial world. The colonies of Spain in Spanish America and Asia, the colonies of Portugal in Brazil, Africa, and Asia, and later those of England in Africa, India, and China present us with a whole new panorama. The colonial world comes into being. The ecumenes that before the fifteenth century were on a par with Europe become its colonies within a century, so that there remains but one ecumene, one center, ringed by a concentric circle.

The term "ecumene" comes from the Greek word *oikoumene,* which is derived from *oikos,* meaning "house." My home is my ecumene, and my home is my world; it is where things take on meaning for me. Someone coming from the outside does not know the significance of the objects in my home, the pictures on the wall or the portrait of my grandfather; that person cannot grasp the meaning of "my home"; I am in charge in my own home because I am in the center and I have always been there.

"World" in the gospel is *kosmos,* and Jesus speaks of the "prince of this *world*"; this prince is completely at home. Every ecumene has its prince and it is about that "prince" that we want to speak.

Totality as Flesh or "My World"

Ecumene is the same as "totality," a highly abstract technical term. "Totality" obviously comes from "total"; we say: "the totality of meaning" of my day-to-day world, because everything in that world has meaning. What is in my world makes sense for me but it would not necessarily do so for another. My world is a totality of meaning; therefore whoever understands the meaning of all that takes place there has to be someone in the *center* of the world. One who is on the periphery of the world does not know what it is all about. This means that the totality has a center, and that center is where everything acquires meaning; in the Bible, totality is called "the flesh." The "sin of the flesh" has nothing to do with the body and much less with the sexual or sensual. The "sin of the flesh" is evil itself, it is a world become totality; it occurs, for example, when an ecumene sees itself as the only ecumene in the world and denies the existence of all others; it occurs when I think only of myself and deny the existence of others; in its essence it is egoism. "Flesh," then, in the Bible means "totality." In the flesh and in the world everything is seen in the light of "this" world; I am the center of that light.

In the age of Hispanic discovery the European world expanded and other human experiences (Mayan, Aztec, Incan, African, Arabian, Hindu, Chinese) were conquered and destroyed.

One example: the Aztecs sacrificed people to the god Huitchilopotli at Tenochtitlán, because in the fifth age of the world a lesser god, the sun, sacrificed himself for others and now the sun needed the blood of humans to subsist. According to the Aztec theology of Tlacaelel the sun-god needed human blood and the Aztecs would have to get victims for the sun-god; for this reason they built an empire. A theologian causes the founding of an empire. What are we to make of this? Well, what more befits a person's dignity: to die sacrificed as a person on the altar of the sun-god or to die in the depths of a mine sacrificed to the gold-and-silver-god like a beast of burden? Many more Indians were sacrificed to the new modern European god than to the Aztec god, and it is far more indecent to die in the depths of a mine like an animal than to die as a divine victim on an altar, even though it be the altar of a false god.

The first bishop of Potosí, of La Plata, quickly censured for theological reasons those who were sacrificing people to the god of gold. Often the Spaniards wanted only to get rich. Spaniards who in Spain were nobodies, menials whose masters were constantly ordering them about, come now to America as conquistadors and want to be the "masters" here—to get rich and go home to Spain, wealthy, in order to say, "I have become rich," a process which later will be called "making it in America." This "making it in America" was achieved with the blood of Indians. That bishop was seeing, as did Bartolomé de las Casas, the new plan of worldwide totalization: Europe's determination to have wealth coming in from overseas; this wealth would have to flow in toward the *center*. Thus arose the gold and silver adventurers, and Spain was the first to begin the quest for wealth and glory. Today in Seville there is a tower that is still called "the tower of gold," where the American gold and silver was deposited and little by little was distributed in Spain until it finally found its way to the rest of Europe in the process of buying manufactured goods, coming to rest in the Low Countries or in London banks. Or it would take the Mediterranean route to Venice and Genoa and from there to the Arab world, coming to rest in China. The Chinese sold silk and spices and bought gold in order to build their temples. It is much more fitting that gold end as a temple ornament than in a bank, and more so because it was purchased through the skilled labor of the Chinese, whereas the gold and silver that came from America had been stolen at the cost of Indian blood.

What is far worse, however, is that that light which illumines all that happens in the world is in turn considered to be sacred, eternal; and Latin Christians go on from there to say that their culture—which is Christendom—is also sacred, because "God is with us." The Christians who came to rob the Chibchas of their gold were not simply Spaniards with a craving for wealth; they also stood before the Indians as Christians. We see here precisely the sacralization of an ecumene whose sole purpose at bottom is to "be in the money."

Between the feudal person whose purpose was to "be in honor" and the person of the church whose purpose was to "be in holiness" there arose in the ninth century a third person, who was neither feudal nor ecclesial and who lived as a pariah in the city and for this reason was called a *burgher, bourgeois.* In the city, working in various handcrafts and saving money, this person began to build a new culture. The bourgeois person came out on top in the French Revolution in 1789 and replaced the feudal person, the noble, and the monarchy. And thus the new bourgeois humanism triumphed; by the sixteenth century it was getting a big boost from Spain because that country was bringing incredible amounts of money from America to Europe, whereas before very little accumulated capital was available in Latin Christendom.

Beyond that Latin ecumene, beyond the *center,* lay in distant darkness the other ecumenes—the Hindu world, the Chinese, the African. They were far off under the night sky, far from the light of Europe; they were barbarous and blasphemous and had to be civilized: civilization here, barbarity there. All the peoples of the center think that they are "civilized" and that all the rest are "barbarians"; the former step forward to offer the gift of civilization and an education to the unlettered peoples. They see themselves as offering the greatest gift, but in reality they will simply oppress them by imposing their culture upon them and stripping them of their uniqueness. The Indians were "other" than the Spaniards; the Chinese and Hindus were "other" than the English. But their otherness would have to be denied them, rooted out of them, annihilated.

European Expansion

The European expansion of the sixteenth century was not a harmless geopolitical fact but, rather, essentially an ethical fact for the Christian, because there was to be a profound injustice within that expansion. When gold and silver were extracted from America and sent to Europe in quantities five times as great as the gold and ten times as great as the silver that existed in Europe, inflation ran rampant. Within the century many people became poor because ten pieces of silver came to be worth only one. The Arabs, without losing a thing in that century, became poor because the quantity of gold and silver arriving in the Mediterranean basin was so great and its value fell so low. Their fall became evident at the battle of Lepanto, which marked the beginning of the disappearance of the Turks, not because they were less valiant but because inflation was wiping them out. To afford a warship or to pay an army, they had to pay out double or more. But the Turks no longer had gold or silver, whereas the Spaniards and, little by little, the Genoese and Venetians were able to pay hard cash. They conquered the Mediterranean because they had first conquered the Atlantic, which now became the new center. The North Atlantic continues to be the center until now. In that North Atlantic are Russia, the United States, and Europe. Japan and Canada ought to be added also. This is the center, and all the rest is periphery.

Samir Amin, an African economist, who is not Christian but neither is he liberal or Marxist, has written a very interesting book called *Accumulation on a World Level*. The accumulation of capital is a big problem for Christians because it raises the question: How does anyone become rich? It would seem that persons would have to start with a certain amount of capital; if they don't have it, how can they make it grow? And if I have even a small amount of capital—where does it come from? Amin, who, although he is African, considers himself to be on the side of the Latin American economists of the left, shows that world accumulation was produced in the center through economic rape of the colonies. Goods were stolen from the colonies and multiplied in the center; gold and silver were stolen from the Indians and exported to the center, carried to Spain. This system of imports to the center was a part of international trade. Spain in its turn sold oils, wine, products that could be produced there. But the balance of trade was unequal; ten times the wealth was taken from America as was returned. This kind of injustice is sinful. The Spaniards in Peru, in Potosí, or in the north of Argentina who set out to mine gold and send it to Spain were thieves guilty of sin; the Spanish miners ought to have been confessing their grave sin; but nobody stopped to think of the morality of the process taking place before their eyes. The conquistadors or *encomenderos* may have felt legally entitled to the gold and may have cheerfully gone about their work, but they were despoilers nonetheless, thieves sending home goods to the center. This economic rape began when Columbus first arrived in the West Indies and saw that there was no gold there; he captured a few Indians and took them off as slaves. A bishop of Michoacán in Mexico said that "the gold and silver that goes to those empires goes purchased with the blood of Indians and wrapped in their hides." This bishop was clearly aware that the gold was stained. How could it not be stained with the blood of Indians? As if that were not enough, it later becomes stained with African blood. From London and Bordeaux shrewd slave traders sailed for Africa and deceived the poor Africans; they sold them in Cartagena or in the Caribbean for the gold and silver of the Indians, whereupon they could buy merchandise; the holds of their ships filled to overflowing, they would return to Europe.

The original accumulation, which was deposited in newly founded banks, allowed for the industrial revolution. The first capitalistic investments were used to produce luxury products—such as soap, perfume, fabrics—which rapidly increase capital because they are sold at a high markup. An investment of ten gold pieces would double within months, and it was thus that capital grew.

Pirates from England, Holland, and France came to Latin American cities to steal. England as well as Portugal and Holland were poor nations that had no colonies. They began their accumulation of capital by stealing. The origin of the accumulation of the center's capital has been not only robbery but murder as well. This is the original sin for the modern European age. Today in the stock market of New York, stocks and bonds from all over the world are bought and sold on an international scale; the capital involved was first amassed in Europe and England; later it passed over to the United States and Russia. That money is stained by the blood of Indians and wrapped in the hides of blacks and Asians. The Opium War that England waged against China to make the Chinese take to opium (the English were too righteous to want to do so) and to bring prosperity to English business interests was just one more of many rotten deeds committed in the name of English Christianity.

The conquest of America was nothing more than oppression. The subjugation of person by person is the only sin a person can commit. It is the expansion of dominion and the establishment of hatred. It is like the Levite and the priest who encounter a wounded man along the way, in the parable of the Good Samaritan, and, instead of helping him, turn away and quicken their pace. Instead of being ministered to, the other is beaten into submission. Conquest is the annihilation of the other as other; it is the establishment of rule. To rule is to dominate the other. Thus the English, the Spanish, the Dutch would reshape a world dominated by their despotic and oppressive rule. Bartolomé de las Casas said that, where they did not actually kill the Indians, they subjected them to the "hardest, roughest, most horrible servitude." Domination of the other is to reduce him or her to the status of servant; it is precisely the construction of a prison so that one person can rule over another.

"He died under Pontius Pilate," says the Apostles' Creed. It is a very easy thing to read this in the creed and to say, "He died under Pontius Pilate." But who is Pilate today? If I do not know who killed Jesus and why he died, I am not a Christian. But it is up to me now not so much to explain how he died under Pontius Pilate but why Pontius Pilate is the Evil One from whom we must be liberated. "Deliver us from the Evil One" is my topic, the world order which from the sixteenth to the twentieth centuries evolved into Soviet-American peaceful co-existence—that is my topic. After certain ominous differences between Soviet Russia and the United States, they have now arrived at "peaceful coexistence"; there are no longer major problems between them. There are other world problems today. The Soviet-American peace indicates an alliance of the center. Europe will still fight for a while against the United States. The Europeans produce the Concorde, a fantastic plane; they sell the Volkswagen to the Americans, and Ford suffers. But all will be straightened out. Japan and Canada are also part of the center. But the battle between them never gets out of hand; they don't shoot to kill each other. But they do kill the peoples on the periphery; the wars have been exported to other places to be fought by the "barbarians."

Germany, Italy, and Japan were industrial nations that wanted in to the center, but because the center would not admit them, they started World War II. Although they lost the war, they won a place in the center thanks to the United States (remember "the German miracle," "the Japanese miracle," and the amazing development of Italy). Since the end of that war (1945) the center has closed in on itself, leaving no room for any other nation because, if the underdeveloped nations were allowed to come in, the high standard of living of those within the center would be lowered considerably. Indeed, there is today a world order, a peaceful coexistence, but dominated by the center over the periphery. And the worst thing about that order is that it has been divinized. For example, Hitler said, *"Gott ist mit uns"* (God is with us). Hitler took unto himself the role of God; and printed on the U.S. dollar bill is the sentence "In God we trust." Everything they do is in the name of God. There are those among us who still defend "western Christian civilization." They take it upon themselves to be God's defenders; this means, of course, that they see themselves as defenders of Christ. They are like a sacrament because their decision-making becomes divinized, a ploy the conqueror uses so that the world order will not be disturbed. For this reason they have to proclaim that "God is with us" and whoever is against that order of domination is against God. The Romans operated in the very same way. The Roman empire and the emperor were divine. Pontius Pilate was therefore the spokesman for God in Palestine and also, but in a different way, so were the priests of the Sanhedrin; both were delegates of God. When Jesus said he was God, there was widespread alarm. The empire, or Pilate, cried out, "If you are God, does that mean I am not?" And the Sanhedrin was scandalized. If you are God and we who are his agents do not know you, this means you are lying. They murdered Jesus for having blasphemed, because they believed themselves to be God, or at least his agents. The order had been divinized. It is only at this concrete level that reflection about theology or about faith begins, in the sense that reflection about faith is theology. If I am not firmly planted in reality, my reflection remains "up in the air"; it is worthless. I tremble when I hear sermons that treat sin in the abstract and allow sinners to feel they are innocent and to think of the innocent poor people as sinners.

The Prophets Against the Idol. The Atheism of Jesus

The theological reflection that I am now proposing is absolutely traditional; it is to be found in the most ancient Judeo-Christian tradition, in the New Testament, and in the whole history of theology. What I have to say at this point will be negative and critical because I am going to talk about the Evil One. Later on we will see how the Evil One operates and why he kills the just; death is the fruit of sin.

This critical method, in its negative phase, begins as do the prophets of Israel, who have a genuine methodology of preaching the liberating vision, revealed to them by God, of the meaning of what is happening.

They always lay out a boundary. This boundary is the world in its totality; it is the flesh; when it is divinized it sees itself as unparalleled and quickly becomes an idol. It believes itself to be God but it is only a god with a small "g." God is the absolute Other, since he is eschatological and therefore does not give himself entirely to us in history but only at the end of history. Thus the prophets, in order to affirm God the Creator, had first to lash out against gods, created by people. For this reason the psalmist says, "Their idols are nothing more than silver and gold"—not without reason does the text say, "silver and gold"—"their idols are products of human skill, have eyes but never see, ears but never hear, noses but never smell, hands but never touch, feet but never walk." Those are the systems that people make and adore; they are their laws, statutes, economic and cultural organizations. All this is the work of humankind but it is called "God." At any rate, it is said that "God is with us and he has blessed us." We have to be careful. It could happen that a bishop or a priest or a layperson identified with the church could give blessing, by simply his or her presence, to an order that is unjust. Woe to that person on the Day of Judgment: Dante stuffed a lot of people in hell in his *Divine Comedy*. Elijah, speaking to the worshipers of Baal, tells them: "Shout louder, since, if it is true that Baal is god, he must be busy or out taking a walk, or maybe he is napping and has to be awakened." Elijah scoffed at these gods. If we dare, we can scoff at these gods also, but we must be prepared to die like Jesus. If we accept these gods as gods, we can get along very nicely, but some day we are going to wake up to the fact that we have been adoring an idol and not God, not Jesus.

This means then that in order to give witness to the Lord, we have to deny the idol, and to deny the idol that purports to be God is atheism with a small "a." The prophets were atheists in regard to false gods and so were the Christians. The Christians who refused to adore the emperor or the state or any other idol or false god were dragged to the arena as atheists and put to death as atheists. Only if I am an atheist in regard to that god can I testify to the God who is Creator; if I deny God the Creator, then I become divine. There are only two possibilities, not three. Atheism itself is not wrong; it is a matter of saying to what God I am being atheistic. Unjust and dehumanizing atheism is the Atheism of the "God-Other," Atheism with a capital "A." The atheism of the idol is spelled with a small "a." We can love God the Creator only if we are atheists in regard to the false god, the idol. Atheism then is not the problem.

Let us consider a text that comes not from a theologian but from an economist—although a theologian could not phrase the matter in a better form: "Criticism of heaven thus becomes criticism of the earth; criticism of religion becomes criticism of law; criticism of theology becomes criticism of politics." Someone might say, "This man totally lacks any religious sense!" But if one can make a god out of the system, one can also make a religion out of the system. When the Romans adored the emperor, they were being faithful to their religion and adoring their gods. Thus, when I say that criticism of heaven is criticism of the earth, I am saying something enormously prophetic. If I do not look critically at the religion of the emperor, I will fail to see the injustices that are committed in the empire, on earth. Criticism of religion is criticism of the earth and criticism of theology is political criticism, because in politics there is sin, which is the domination of person over person. There is a cultural theology that justifies this, seeing the dominator as a god.

We Christians tend to get very upset when an intellectual says, "I am an atheist." But we should right away ask, "In regard to what God?" Jesus and the prophets were atheists in regard to false gods. "Give to Caesar what is Caesar's and to God what is God's." Jesus, then, was an atheist in regard to Caesar. Jesus began to criticize the religion of the Romans and of the temple to bring about a new alignment with the "God-other," which was himself. I mean that there are two religions—that of the idol and that of the God of Israel, the saving Creator. Therefore, the text of the economist just quoted quickly becomes a theological text and what he says is soundly orthodox: "The original accumulation comes to play, in political economy, the same role that original sin plays in theology." This means that to accumulate capital, a capitalist robs the Indians and the blacks. But it is worse than that. It is the center that, in robbing Indians and killing blacks, produces that accumulation. Somebody's death—original injustice—is the origin of accumulation. Five centuries ago it was precisely the desire for gold and silver—"Their idols are no more than gold or silver," said the prophets—that led them into sin, the sin of human domination. And this author goes on to say that "in the period of manufacturing the prime concern of commerce was industry. The colonial system therefore played the dominant role in those times. It was indeed *a foreign god.* . . ."

The author of these lines is Jewish. Obviously he is being prophetic without realizing it. He is also unaware that he is really Judeo-Christian in his outlook. Speaking of that money back in the period of manufacturing, he says: "It was a foreign god which came to be enthroned on the altar, together with the ancient gods of Europe, a god which one fine day would have them all bowing and scraping." This is to say that that money that came from the colonies was going to be much more powerful than all the other little gods of the pantheon.

It comes to this: It is perfectly right to be an atheist as far as idols are concerned. But one who is not sufficiently alert can fall into an error that Marx, almost inevitably, fell into—the error of denying the idol without affirming the "God-Other." The danger, then, is of attempting to construct a perfect system, without contradictions. If I divinize such a system, I am allowing for bureaucratic domination that is above all criticism. This is what happened in Russia.

Marx is not heterodox because he is an atheist (in regard to the idol, to money). He is heterodox because he is not enough of an atheist, because in his failure to affirm the "God-other" he is left with a system that has no outside support and no radical critique. Christianity is atheistic in regard to every idol—this it shares with Marx; but it is more critical than Marx because, in affirming the "God-other," it is critical of every *possible* system and will be until the eschatological times, until the end.

Although people believe Marx to be intelligent—and he was—they do not know that Jesus is even more intelligent, that he goes far beyond Marx because his method is more critical.

Sin as a Totalization of the System

Sin, all sin, is by nature a totalization. When we sin, we think we are all that there is and are therefore divine. We deny the Other and believe that our own totalized order is the kingdom of heaven. Those who would say, "I am in the kingdom" are really in sin. Those who know and believe that the kingdom is not only *here* but also *yet to come* has the kind of readiness and openness that will enable them to receive Jesus in the Parousia. Those who think they already have it "in their pocket" and consider it their own will be told by the returning Lord, "I do not know you." Nobody has Jesus in their pocket; no one is yet in the eternal All. We have one foot in and the other out, in such a way that there is a now but also a not-yet. And the not-yet is basic, because the true kingdom comes later. This means then that sin, paradoxically, is to totalize, and to totalize is to create an idol. And this is evil, the only kind of evil.

That original evil is exactly what is described in the four symbolic accounts in the first eleven chapters of Genesis. A symbolic account is a myth in the sense that a myth is an account of reality that is expressed rationally in symbolic form, valid for all people and for all epochs. These myths, in a way, are a message that God has for humanity—not only for primitives but also for persons who land on the moon and who work with computers.

The first and most concrete myth is that of Cain and Abel; the second and most abstract is that of Adam. The next two are less important—those of Noah and of Babel. Each one treats a different aspect of evil.

Beginning with the first myth, we learn that Cain was in his world, and Abel in his. And Cain killed Abel. Cain was an urbane city-dweller, whereas Abel was a shepherd. The shepherd's way with things is to wander about like an outsider, whereas the city-dweller takes over as if an owner of the whole earth.

Thus there was outright rivalry between prophetism, which is nomadic like Abraham, and the Canaanites, who were influential in getting the Jews to live in cities and to worship the baals, the idols. It is a problem of poverty and wealth. The sedentary person—the possessor—is the person of the city, Cain; on the other hand, the poor shepherd who walks the earth a free person is Abel. The latter is the attitude we must always have; it is what the prophets have. The person who is free can adore God.

Cain killed Abel; he killed a brother, the Other. Upon killing the Other he committed fratricide. Every fratricide since the Incarnation has amounted to theocide. Theocide is a prevalent notion at the moment in European thought; the "death of God" is often spoken of. It was Nietzsche who said, "God is dead." Like the genius that he was, he pointed out that "Our hands are stained with the blood of God." In effect, to kill the brother is to kill the epiphany of God; it is not as if God died but that he disappeared, because Abel—"Holy Abel" as Jesus called him—is the poor person in the Beatitude sense of the word "poor." Abel is the epiphany of the absolute Other, of God.

In biblical thought are two basic categories; the first is totality, or flesh, and the second—essential for understanding the whole Bible—is the Other, who is not only God but also the other brother by our side. Jesus once asked, "Who is in the neighborhood?" In the New Testament this is ordinarily translated, "Who is my neighbor?" Jesus answers with a parable. Do not believe that Jesus was a simple or ignorant man, a moralist for the crowd. Jesus was a Hebrew theologian who had a method, the method of the prophets, and he used this theological method with perfect preciseness.

The theology born later in the West was not in accordance with the Hebrew method. When Jesus was asked who was the perfect person and who the poor person, he taught them the parable of the Good Samaritan. There was a man lying wounded along the side of the road, the Other, the poor man; he had been assaulted. There passed by the Other a Levite, who, because he was so totalized, so wrapped up in his affairs, saw nothing. He was totalized, his flesh was blocked off, he was in sin. Later a priest came by, so absorbed in his worries that he did not see the poor man either. Lastly a Samaritan —utterly despised by the Jews—came along. The Samaritan was also flesh, totality, but although he rode a mule and carried possessions and money with him, he was open, he was able to establish the original experience of Judeo-Christianity, the face-to-face. Therefore he accepted the fact that the wounded man was the Other, that he was worthy of being ministered to. The Samaritan's service is the fulfillment of Christian existence, as it was in the beginning and will be until the kingdom of heaven comes. In the kingdom there will be no theoretical vision but a face-to-face, which is something much more profound. We are confronted here with one of the great distortions of Christian thought—the distortion of no longer knowing the meaning of the face-to-face experience, the kind of experience one has with a loved person. This is the highest form of wealth, beauty, joy, happiness—to be face-to-face with her, with him. "Moses was face-to-face before God." In Hebrew, when a word is used twice, the meaning is intensified, much as we might say, "Years and years ago."

Face-to-face indicates proximity; "Moses was mouth-to-mouth with God." And in the Song of Songs, the loved one cries out, "Let him kiss me with the kisses of his mouth." Face-to-face, mouth-to-mouth is the fundamental experience through which I respect the Other as other, I love the Other as other; it is *agape*. Charity is not merely friendship among brothers, because then it would be a totalized *we,* a house tightly closed. It would not be charity, love for the Other as other, for John says, "He *first* loved us." The one who loves first does not yet have friendship, because to love the Other as other comes before the love is returned. Friendship is mutual well-wishing, allowing us to be self-centered. To love the Other without receiving the Other's love is not mutual well-wishing but pure well-wishing toward the Other. It does not matter whether the Other reciprocates—I love that person for himself; only this makes it possible for that person to love me some day. This is how friendship really comes about. Charity is not merely comradeship, it is love freely given. How can parents come to love a child? Before the child was begotten, it did not exist. The parents love the child *before* they have it and that is *why* they have it. Procreation is similar to creation. God creates us while we are still unable to love him. He stands before us face-to-face, in the sense of love for the Other as other and not just as one of us. To see others as just one of us may be a kind of group selfishness; it is not love. Love for the Other as other is charity, *agape;* it is a revealed concept found only in Judeo-Christianity, the most revolutionary approach to love in all history.

Cain was face-to-face with Abel and killed him. His action was just the opposite of the Samaritan's. The Samaritan was of service to the wounded man, and "service" is a technical word in Hebrew. Upon killing Abel, Cain was left alone. After killing the Other, who was there to reveal the Word of God to him? The Word of God in our lives comes to us only from the Other. If you tell me that the Word is in the Bible or in the liturgy, I shall believe it, but all I want to say here is that we are touched by the Word only when a poor person summons us. (The church also summons us as the Other.) I can read lovely Bible texts from the depths of my sinful totalization, and thus can, with my false approach, become more and more divinized. But someone suddenly charging into my world and telling me, "I have rights that are not yours" upsets me, disconcerts me, challenges me, demands that I go "beyond" myself. That which makes me go beyond is service. "The Servant of Yahweh," Jesus, practiced that kind of service. So, if I kill Abel, I am alone, I am unparalleled, and thus I am a god. It is a fratricide coupled with pantheism, because I divinize myself as the Unparalleled One. And at the same time it is an apparent theocide of God the Creator. This *is* the sin of Adam. The rational structure of the Cain-and-Abel myth is rather simple, but that of Adam is a bit more complex.

The Sin of Adam

While dwelling in the innocence of paradise, Adam ate the fruit of the "tree of life." This wanting to eat "life" is wanting to be God. ("Life" is the life of the All, divine life, the life of the gods; it is as though one would have the Promethean fire of the gods that the gods did not want humans to have.) Wanting to eat of the tree of life is not so much a sin of pride as it is of idolatry and pantheism. "Adam," meaning humanity as such—we are all "Adam" when we wish to eat of the tree of life—wishes to be God, but in order to be God he has to be the Unparalleled One. This means he must kill the other through some kind of injustice. This is why the prophets say, "There is no God because there is no justice." I can deny God only when I have killed the brother and, in order that my religious conscience not reproach me for his death, I have to affirm myself as God. Once everything is divine, injustice also appears to be perfectly natural.

In Latin America many people say the poor are poor because they are lazy and will not work. This judgment is an original sin. They will not accept that the poor are lazy not because they want to be but because they are the victims of a system whose benefits go to those making this judgment. This bourgeois argument that you hear constantly hides the fact of human and historical injustice and, in doing so, sets up injustice as though it were of divine origin, a natural fact over which we have no control. In this way Pilate washes his hands. The prince of this world becomes the natural law. A great contemporary Jewish thinker and philosopher has said: "War comes to be very reasonable."

Heraclitus, who was not given to being vague, said, "War is the start of everything." If war, then, is the start of everything, this means that injustice is natural. This is exactly what the story of Adam denies. Adam sins and the Bible makes the point that it was his free decision, that evil is not divine but human. In declaring God to be innocent, the Bible blames humankind for all sin. The cause is human freedom and the prince of this world, that is, the Devil. I had a Scripture professor who confessed that he "could not prove the existence of the Devil but he believed in him." But the essential point is that humankind is also the prince of this world. It would be untrue to think that there is only a demonic person to blame, a fallen angel out there on whose shoulders we can place all our sins and be free of them.

Nor can we put the blame entirely on him for our temptations. People also can be "the prince of this world." An individual goes to a broker's office and says, "I want my investment to net me 5 percent instead of 3 percent annually." The broker replies, "Put your investment in an armaments company stock. They have a higher yield." The following year the broker can very proudly say, "There you are! A 5 percent profit on your investment." "Nice going," says the investor. But the investment helped pay for arms that killed people. That doesn't make any difference to the "princes of this world," who matter-of-factly kill people for economic benefits. They are Cains who kill Abel, Adams who eat of the tree of life and become gods, unparalleled, no Other before them.

God told Noah that, because people had done evil, he was going to destroy them. Noah floated safely on the ark of faith while all other people were destroyed. This tells us that the idol will reign for a time but that it will be destroyed. The destruction of the Beast in the book of Revelation will be like that of Sodom and Gomorrah. All the *systems* of sin in history will end up dead, and the dead will be buried with the dead. Those who play by the system will lose their lives in the system. "But you, follow me," to be of *service* to Abel instead of killing him. Sin sowed a confusion of tongues at Babel, whereas the one who searches out the poor will be understood perfectly and will "converge." One thinks of the Latin American brand of ecumenism between Protestants and Catholics who fight for the poor; they "converge" in their liberation efforts. It is a kind of ecumenism very different from that of the Old World.

This, then, is what I mean by the Evil One. The Evil One is the totalization of a system that negates the poor. The Indians, Africans, and Asians were negated; the poor, the farmers, the laboring class go on being negated within these systems. Another name for the Evil One is Pontius Pilate. Let us not forget that he was a delegate of the empire. The very idea of alienation is implicit in the notion of empire. The concept and the word "alienation" are very Christian when used in reference to Christ—He "emptied himself" (Phil. 2:7). To alienate the other means that Indians with their world, their possessions, their culture are transformed into tools in the hands of the Spaniards; the blacks, who had their world, were alienated from it and sold into slavery. Alienation is to kill the other; it is to kill Abel. You make the other dependent, at someone else's beck and call. You make the other a thing. The Indian is of value to the European, the person in the center, only as a trained thing. This world order becomes fixed and even claims to be eternal, natural and, furthermore, divine. This fixing of the prevailing order is Evil. The conquest was bad enough but worse still is the claim to be eternal of the established order. This brings us to the question of inheritance.

We know, of course, that the system of Spanish land grants came under heavy fire. Therefore King Charles of Spain, in the New Laws of 1542, proposed that the land grants not be hereditary. In this way the Indians could recover their freedom within a generation. But the proposal met with stiff resistance in Mexico, Central America, Peru, and all over. The New Laws faded from existence. Land grants went on being hereditary in the colonial oligarchy. This means that if the conquest and the murder of the other are unjust, even more unjust is the eternalization of the system, of the *institutions* that perpetuate the original sin. So we can say it is just as bad to inherit what is stolen as it is to steal.

Institutional Inheritance of the Sin of Theft

There are three origins of property: (1) I work to get my property; (2) I steal, like the English pirates and the modern Europeans, and in this way I get property; (3) I inherit. There is nothing to justify the last two. Only the first is valid. I rightfully have what I work for and it is always relatively little. If I have a lot, it is because I robbed someone, perhaps without even being aware of it. Later on, my children will inherit my property, and, along with it, my original sin.

How is original sin inherited? Along some hidden channel? No. The mother says to her son: "Don't play with that kid down the street. He's dirty and you might get some disease." Later on, a schoolmate wants to borrow that child's eraser and the son says: "Don't let him have it. You'll never get it back." The son becomes totalized without realizing it, a simple matter of inheriting original sin. When we reach the age of freedom—i.e., thirteen, fourteen years of age—when we are really born, we become aware that we have played the role of Cain many times, killing many Abels unknowingly because that is the way we were brought up. Original sin is transmitted through the ontological constitution of our being in the course of our education. On the day the child is taken from the uterus, it is not in the kingdom but neither is it condemned. The child has the potentiality of being a person, but by adolescence is already in the kingdom of sin because cultural formation has taken place within the institutions of injustice.

There are echoes here, of course, of Rousseau. Rousseau taught the opposite of Calvin and spoke in a very Catholic way when he said: "Man is born neither good nor bad but institutions make him bad." He came close to talking about what the Bible calls "the sin of the world." The sin of the world is the sin of the flesh, and the sin of the flesh is likewise transmitted through cultural conditioning. The fifteen-year-old child of an aristocrat, of an oligarch who despises the poor and seeks only to augment the family wealth, is living in sin and has a share in all the deaths of Abel. Cain is both the agent of the Evil One and the Evil One himself.

"Our Father . . . deliver us from the evil one," "lead us not into temptation." That is the question—for us to be delivered from being one with the prince of this world, from entering knowingly and willingly into the structures of human domination. Deliver us!

When a poor exploited worker comes home and beats his wife, he is also a sinner inasmuch as he is a subjugator of his wife. In spite of the fact that his reaction is fair toward those over him in the factory, he is a sinner toward those who are not at fault—his wife, his child, those he beats up when he is drunk.

It is difficult not to be unjust on some level. But when we are unjust it is precisely because we are caught up in the system determined in history by the princes of this world.

This is the first thesis that I want to propound: the original sin of the prevailing world system has first of all been colonial domination. This is the first sin; all the others in the system spring from it. The greater sins are those that we don't even notice.

And this is the way the devil is present in real history. No one believes in the devil anymore. It is necessary for the devil that no one believe in him. But maybe what happens is that we locate him wrongly. We locate him within the individual conscience where, for example, he might tempt me sexually. This may be important, but not very; the great temptations into which one falls daily are the political and cultural structures of sin. Sin has become a very private affair. But the great historic and communitarian sins of humankind pass unnoticed by all. This is how the prince of this world rules.

2

Theologal Anthropology II: Ethics as Liberation Criticism

> ... *and He died under Pontius Pilate.*
> Apostles' Creed

The Apostles' Creed, the oldest creed in the church, tells us that Jesus died under Pontius Pilate. Just before we come to this phrase in the creed, we read: "We believe ... in one Lord, Jesus Christ; ... by the power of the Holy Spirit he was born of the Virgin Mary; ... he was crucified under Pontius Pilate [and] died."

I would like to show through this text how Jesus breaks through into the flesh, into the structures of sin, and blows them apart, being ground up nevertheless by the prince of this world.

I also would like to go into the thinking of Franz Rosenzweig, who was a German-Jewish theologian at the beginning of the century. I have studied the Jewish theologians in considerable depth because they give a good account of the way things were before the Incarnation; they have a keen insight into pre-Christian happenings that helps one understand the complementariness of the Old Testament to Christianity. Rosenzweig was an extraordinary Jew who was very sick for many years and who, in spite of his constant pain, was able to write a unique book entitled *The Star of Redemption* (New York: Holt, Rinehart & Winston, 1971). In that book he laid down the fundamental categories that Emmanuel Levinas employs. Rosenzweig, commenting on the history of Moses and the exodus, says some beautiful things. I am indebted to his viewpoint in what follows.

Dead Flesh: The Totalized System

The flesh when closed up is dead and its death is sin. When the flesh closes up, it becomes totalized and says: "I am all there is because I have already killed Abel." Totalized flesh—this is the meaning of sin as death. This does not mean, of course, that sinners drop dead. They are alive with biological life, but they are dead as far as human life is concerned because they are subjugated, totalized. Jesus said to Nicodemus, "You must be born again." How? By detotalizing the self, getting out of the flesh, opening up the self. Baptism is the condition of possibility for this detotalization of the system. It is grace.

Thus to "let the dead bury the dead" is to let them lose their lives in their concern for the stystem. The bourgeois person of our world today works in order to have more and more money. Such a person is a lackey of the devil, who goes about burying the dead. But Jesus says to us, "You, follow me."

Just as dead as totalized flesh is divinized totality because it believes itself to be God; it is the idol. It is that Totality that Otherness breaks into.

In the beginning we stated: "We believe in Jesus Christ who was born of the Holy Spirit." The Other is the *Holy One*. Poor people are holy ones inasmuch as they are outside the system; such persons are innocent of all the sins of the system because they have not committed them but have been their victim. God is the Other, the Holy of holies, the Saint of saints.

From "outside" the totalization of sin and of the flesh, from the Spirit, the Word breaks into the world. But how can the Word seep into the flesh if the flesh remains closed up? If the flesh is totalized in sin because I am constantly watching to see how my stock-market investments are doing, the Word cannot enter. Only if I do not see myself as being all there is, only if I have a deep and constant respect for Abel can I then be open to Abel. In this case I am the Samaritan who takes the poor person off to be healed. This openness to the Other, which is always and in concrete instances openness to the poor and through them to God, is the giving of food to whoever asks me for food. There are not three possibilities but only two: Yes or no. "If you did not give food to this poor person, you did not give me food . . . and therefore I do not know you"—this could be said to us at the Judgment. Those who open themselves to the Other say, like Mary, "Be it done unto me." This is perfect flesh, the perfect creature.

Quite suddenly we have tied in a mariological reflection with the entire European colonization of America —Mary is the *flesh* which opens up: "Be it done unto me according to your *Word.*" She is the liberation Virgin, she is the Virgin of Guadalupe carried by the Indians at the vanguard of the army of Padre Hidalgo who fought, in 1809, against the Mexican oligarchy and Spanish power with the battlecry, "The land for those who work!" This is the Virgin who said: "He has pulled down princes from their thrones and exalted the lowly." It can be said that she was in favor of subverting law and order! But was not her Son put to death for being a subversive? Without realizing that Jesus was put to death as a subversive by the empire and the traitorous oligarchy of his country, we cannot understand what happened in what we call Holy Week.

"Be it done unto me, according to your Word." This means that the flesh becomes open and for that reason the Incarnation takes place. "In-carnation" (the process of taking on flesh) is something *within* the flesh.

All that I have said is strictly technical; I am not using symbolic approximations but a method. It is a matter of categories, it is the theology of Jesus. In the Incarnation the Eternal Word was in-humanized in the humanity that is totality as flesh. In order for Jesus to become incarnate, to become in-totalized, to enter into this human world, someone had to open the self. Here is where the young girl of Nazareth enters; by the power of the Holy Spirit (strictly and essentially this means that Christ is from absolute Otherness) she conceives Christ in her womb. The Otherness of the Word is absolute and cannot be incarnated through human mediation. From absolute Otherness the Word breaks into the totality of the flesh, and therefore the Incarnation is also the summons of the poor as otherness in the world as a system.

Incarnation as the "Death of Death"

The Other as "exteriority" is definitively God. Whenever we respect the Other as other, we live our lives as we should. Evil enters our lives when we do not respect the Other but use the Other as a *thing*. When I kill Abel I sin; I see him as a thing. If I respect Abel as other, I am the Samaritan who helps, serves, heals, and puts him back on the road to life. The Virgin Mary was so accustomed to respecting the Other as other that when the Absolute Other called upon her, she said, "Be it done unto me." She did not see herself as God; she was an atheist in regard to herself. She never wished to eat of the tree of life because she never wanted to be God. She knew that God was the Other and thus it was easy for her to *open herself*. Jesus is the mysterious *bringing together* of the divine Otherness and the human Totality. This mystery of a bringing together is the first thing the Bible talks about when it reveals to us that "In the beginning God created the heavens and the earth." This is to say that the Other created the totality, the flesh. For this reason John begins his Gospel in the same way but at another level. Because John was Jewish, he intended to begin his Gospel with praise to the Word of God and thus he was inspired to turn to the prophets. In the beginning it was the creative Word, but now it is the re-creative Word: " In the beginning was the Word (*logos*). . . . The Word was made *flesh*."

Not only did God create everything but he re-created it. This re-creation is Jesus. Jesus, the countenance of God, is a person of God. He is the divine person who manifests himself in history; being of flesh, of the world, he reconciles everything. He is the *countenance* that is born of the Virgin by the power of the Holy Spirit. He is the Word of God who can now speak for the poor of the world from flesh and to flesh (the system). The Word on becoming flesh, that is, on gaining entry into the system, upset the totalized totality. He, as a divine Person, essentially Other, Other beyond any system, will always remain within the system and also, like a breach, outside it. The kingdom will now be a "within" with no "outside," since in the outside there is a future and the kingdom is the ultimate (in Greek: *eschatos,* whence comes the word "eschatology"). The kingdom rises up like a historic invasion of the eschatological—which means that Christ permeates the whole system to thrust everything forward. Christ unhinges the hinge of the system where everyone treads the usual path of sin. The Word is infleshed in order to blow apart the hinge. He unhinges everything in order to set up new hinges. From old hinges to new hinges (which are new totalizations of sin) to new liberations, there are new systems and new sins needing continual liberation until the end of time. It is the death of death.

The Paschal Incarnation of Liberation

The Incarnation is the invasion of the Otherness of God who is always Other, an eschatological invasion because it is the ultimate thrust that puts into liberating motion all systematization. But Jesus invades totality in a determined place, not just anywhere. We are told: "Having the divine condition, he emptied himself, taking the form of a slave." The better word, of course, is servant, but not in the sense we think of when the Hebrew refers to the "servant" of Yahweh. The "servant" here is the one who carries out the provident plan of God; it is *service* in regard to the poor; it is work in regard to the needy and to God. In fact we can say that work for God is nothing more than work for the poor. "Service" is the same thing. The priests of the temple performed the "services," the divine rites. They would take an animal and sacrifice it solely to God. As for the poor, they would bake a chicken in the oven and give it to whoever was hungry. If I dismember an animal and burn it in the name of God, I perform a divine sacrifice. Work in service of the poor is *worship* of the poor and a prime condition for the acceptance of worship of God. I must first serve the poor and in them God. The second step is unacceptable without the first. "I desire mercy and not sacrifices." This means that if I exploit the Indian, I cannot very well take part in the Mass later on. If I sell

African slaves, the same is true because the poor are the epiphany of the living God.

Jesus took the "form of a servant," a poor person. The rich are the rulers and the poor are always the ruled. Again, let there be no doubt that Jesus took the form of the poor person. We ought now to explicate a question that is heavily debated among us.

The "poor" in one sense are the oppressed. But there are three meanings to the word "poor." "Poor" is the servant as dominated, ruled. Jesus was not an "intellectual" who had studied in a school of theology or in the temple of Jerusalem as did Paul. The poor Jesus was a man of the land, of the people. How is it that he knows so many things if he has had no teachers? object those who despise him. But Jesus, not only through infused knowledge but also through the education that he received in the synagogue at Nazareth, learned the theological categories of his people and brought them to their culmination, because his intellect was not encumbered with the limitations of sin. He thought more clearly than anyone. Therefore when he was a child of twelve and the priests asked him about the traditions of his people to see if he was ready to take his place as an adult in the community, he surprised them because he put things in a way that disconcerted them. It was as if a boy today in catechism class would say that the unjust sale of raw materials was a sin. Jesus saw the deep and mysterious relationships of sin and the historical liberation of his people in relation to the history of all other peoples. They were amazed because, having taken the radical stance of a poor man among his people, he had understood the mystery. He not only took on the "condition of a servant" but accepted that condition unreservedly—accepting death itself (Phil. 2:5).

Why did Jesus die on the cross? Was it because the

heavenly Father was a sadist? This is a gross error. Jesus did not come to pay a debt, nor by any means did he come to compensate for the sufferings that the Father would have experienced. On the other hand, the Father accepted that he would live the logic of sin, and, living this logic within himself, he would bring about the definitive destruction of the system of sin, that is, he would conquer with his death the death of sin and thus arrive at Resurrection.

The "passage from death to life" also means the passage from one system to another more just, the greatest of all—the kingdom of heaven. It is the passage from oppression to liberation: "I have seen my people enslaved in Egypt," and God tells Moses, "Free them."

This passage from death to life is a movement of conquest. The word "passage" means pasch. Before the final pasch comes there is to be a historical passage—the passage from Egypt (which is also called the "departure from Egypt," and departure is exodus: *ex* [from], *hodos* [road]), like a departure from prison. In prison I am a slave; upon my departure I am free. "Exodus" is another way of saying liberation. In Isaiah 61 we read: "The spirit [the Spirit of Otherness] . . . has been given to me; he has sent me to bring good news to the poor, . . . to proclaim a year of favor from Yahweh, . . . to proclaim liberty to captives."

The word "liberation," so upsetting to many people, is perfectly biblical and Christian: "Father, deliver, liberate them from the Evil One. . . ."

The pasch is the passage that is celebrated as a feast of joy—the Eucharist. The Eucharist is the feast of the liberation from Egypt; it is the feast of the Paschal Lamb before the deliverance, it is what people feel when they see they have been freed from slavery; it is redemption; it is salvation. Jesus redeems; it is like getting out of prison.

Redeemers are those who hand themselves over so that the prisoners can go free. Redemption is exactly the work of the servant: it is a service by which the Samaritan helps the poor man to become a new person: He takes him out of slavery, he frees him.

The Three Meanings of "Poor"

There are three meanings to the word "poor." In the first place, poor means oppressed—Jesus took the position of the oppressed.

In the second place, the poor are the prophets who bear the lot of the poor, "the servants of Yahweh." The prophets are poor because when they speak to totality in the name of the poor they stand alone. Because the prophets advocate an order that will be more just for the poor, they are killed. Witnesses to a future order are saying that the present order is dying, because if there is to be a new order, the old must disappear. The Devil, who is "the prince of this world," cannot tolerate the death of death (that is, the death of the fossilized totality). Before the system dies, the system kills the witness. Therefore the martyrs die; and therefore John writes the book of Revelation to show that the martyrs of the Roman empire are the builders of the heavenly Jerusalem, and that their blood is the building material. The martyrs' blood is the same as the blood of Jesus.

Those who give witness to the future affirm the death of the present order and become a sign of contradiction for the system. The sign is at one and the same time historical and eschatological. Historically, to pass from one order to another, it has been necessary for the subjugators to cease subjugating; without their wealth, they could even stop sinning. But before being dispossessed the subjugators would rather give up their lives, so identified are they with the Devil, who will do anything to avoid ceding power. The salvation of the subjugators, of the sinners, is brought about by the liberation of the poor, because once the former lose the instruments of subjugation, they are no longer capable of sin. "The rich" who lost their wealth during political upheavals and were reduced to being office workers, poor laborers, very likely were saved by what was done to them. So let us not be scandalized by those who take away private property; they may well represent the hand of God reaching out to save the subjugators.

The third meaning of poor is those who are outside the system, oppressed *and* outside the system. A poor man on a cold day walks by the window of a rich man and sees him and his wife and children sitting down in comfort to a nice steak dinner. The other is *outside* in the cold and saying, "God, how lucky *they* are!" He is viewing the system from outside; *they* are within and they view from within. Like gods they are living in a well-established order. The well-established and closed-off system is sin. That is, the poor man views from outside the order that is not his; he yearns for an order that he would be part of, a future order like the kingdom of heaven. Even those poor who are ignorant of Jesus want this. Whereas those who are well installed within the order want it to remain that way forever: "The kingdom is on earth." This is humanity's sin.

The Hebrew word for "work" and "worship" is the same. The work of liberation is the same as the service of the Servant; it is the same as the worship of God. The worship of God is a liberating praxis of the poor, but it is a praxis that does not arise from pure necessity, and it is not a praxis of domination.

Toward a Christian Ethic of Liberation

The subjugators employ a praxis; it is an act by which they subjugate. The subjugators pay people just enough so they will not leave the factory. But let them unionize and declare a strike and they are fired. Today we rarely see management providing labor schools for their workers so that they will understand what their rights are. Even where this is done, it reeks of paternalism and is another form of subjugation.

There is, furthermore, a praxis of necessity: I do something because I need to do it. I go to the bakery to buy bread because I need to eat bread. But just as *service* is not a praxis of subjugation, neither is it of necessity. Rather, it is a praxis of gratuity; it occurs when I do something for the Other as other, not because I need to, since I already have food. It is the other who needs food. When I do something for the Other as other, that is the praxis of liberation. It has to do with liberating the Other as other because to eat bread is an equivocal act. The purpose of eating bread is to subsist; it is an act of possession. And thus I can eat bread so that later on I can go to the stock market and trade; or I can eat bread just to subsist, which is not good either, or I can eat in order to have enough energy to serve the Other, to give my life for the Other, and this is the only good human act. So the real question is not the eating of bread but the *why* of it. The only really good act is the act directed to the Other as other, and every other act is either indifferent or evil.

There were times when Christian ethics tried to tell us that the foundation of morality was the end—beatitude, happiness. The end is also the purpose of the established order. But if I fulfill the end of an established order of subjugation, I commit sin. The end of an established order is not, simply because it is established, the foundation of a good act. I can live up to the constitution of a nation and end up in hell because the national constitution can be totally evil. It does me no good to cry out, "I have complied with the law," because laws can be unjust. Outlaws can really be good. This is what happened to Jesus and that is why he said, "The law was made for man and not man for the law." When people put themselves outside the law, they are out in the cold. Again, this happened to Jesus. When he proposed a new order, the old order became an unjust imposition.

At times, to be good we must flout the law, so that we may fulfill the law of loving the Other as other, a love that goes beyond all law. How risky it is to be a Christian! No wonder the prophet, understanding finally what his role was to be, cried out, "Cursed be the day I was born!" as if to say, "Why has such a dangerous calling been given to me? It will cost me my life, just as it did for Jesus." "The cross" is not a form of self-laceration I inflict upon myself because in my comfortable middle-class condition I don't have sufficient pain. This would be nothing more than masochism and would have nothing to do with sanctity. It is often a striving for perfection without renouncing the prince of this world. But if we put ourselves in the place of Jesus we will be lacerated, not by ourselves but by the sin of the world. Penitential practices can easily be a form of vice and this may very well have been the case in medieval monasteries. But when, like the saints, we try to subvert the reigning order, we will be beaten and the lashes will be administered by our own brothers, as happened in the case of St. Bernard, St. Francis, or St. John of the Cross.

Again, current laws cannot be the foundation of the good act, because laws are nothing more than the exigencies of the end. To achieve a certain end, well-defined means are necessary. The end is the foundation of law;

but if the end is bad, the law is unjust, and if I comply with an unjust law, my act is bad, it is a sin. I would be better off not complying with the law.

Furthermore, the prevailing virtues can be habits of subjugation, because those who subjugate everything determine what is virtuous. Thus the prevailing virtues do not serve us as a guide to what is a good action because they are the virtues of subjugation and not of liberation.

The prevailing values, all told, are only the prevailing values of the subjugating group.

Liberating praxis has its origin from the Other as other. It is service to the poor who are outside the system, who are beyond the ends and the laws of the system. Today it means serving the peoples on the periphery, wanting the liberation of those peoples. When we want, and commit ourselves to, the liberation of the peoples of Latin America, we enter into salvation history. Thus when the Chinese people broke out of their dependence on the Russians, they put themselves on this road, the road of service to the poor. Jesus fulfills this service when he commits himself to the poor and says, "Blessed are you," which was to announce their liberation from all systems. Among the Hindus the poor are the pariahs, the lowest of the castes; they are those who do not comply with the order. The Rig Veda so arranged things as to immobilize the system, the flesh. In the same way, Confucius ingeniously established an order that lasted from his time—the seventh century before Christ—until the Chinese revolutions of 1912 and 1949. In India and China there was no one who could budge the established order because it was understood that to defy the order was wrong. The Devil imposes an unjust order and judges anyone who violates it to be evil. But Jesus turns this completely around. Jesus says that the pariahs are the blessed ones, the highest caste, well beyond the law.

He thus becomes a subversive in regard to the unjust order because he sacralizes the poor, whereas Confucius sacralized the order. Jesus proposes a kingdom that is beyond all historical order, because it is an eschatological kingdom. Thus, without having drawn a sword, he makes every subjugator tremble, beginning with Herod. This is why Herod wanted to kill the infant Jesus. Jesus was born as one already crucified. They persecuted him from birth because he came to announce a kingdom in which the poor would be blessed.

If the order is sacralized, there is no one who can touch it; therefore, if there is no possibility of a new historical order in the future, God the Creator is denied, the kingdom of heaven is denied, the Spirit is denied.

The Logic of Sin

Only now can we understand the statement, "He died under Pontius Pilate." He died "crushed like a grape in the wine press." Why did Herod want to kill the infant Jesus? Why did the Roman soldiers torture and mistreat him and gouge his side with a lance? Did the oppressed make those lances? No. Arms are made in armament factories. They are the only arms that torture and rip open the heart of Jesus. Frightening though it is, there is a logic of sin, a logic of totality, a logic of the flesh. It is the realm of human will as the realm of sin. It is the logic of the realm of this world that inevitably had to kill Jesus, because Jesus, being the Son of God and of Mary, was such a clear sign that the structure of sin had no doubt that he had to be eliminated. We are sinners and in the half light of our wrongdoing sin does not see us as clearly its opposite and therefore it leaves us with our life. But if we were clearly anti-sin, we would be so intolerable for the order of sin that it would destroy us.

The logic of sin is this: The Other, who is Abel, is killed or treated as a thing: subjugated. If the victim is unaware of this subjugation, there is peace, as in the Soviet-American peaceful coexistence. If a people that is subjugated believes that this subjugation is by eternal decree and that God is in favor of it, all goes well for the established order. But if all of a sudden someone preaches to the poor that they are blessed, that the kingdom of heaven is theirs, that they have dignity, that they can be free, that there is an order in which they can be fully humans and they believe the preacher, the subjugators tremble. If the subjugators were to free the poor, they would die as subjugators but would be reborn as saved people. Thus we don't have to kill the brothers or sisters as persons but the subjugators as subjugators. The subjugators become identified with sin when the oppressed start out on the freedom trail toward a new order. So we have to dispossess the subjugators in order to save them.

The prophet starts the process by saying to the poor, "You are poor but free and of great value; you are blessed and yours is the kingdom of heaven." When the poor rise up, they no longer cry out as did Martin Fierro, "Because of my ignorance I know that I am worthless." The subjugators made the poor believe they were worthless; and as long as they believed this, all went well with the established order; but as soon as they rose up and realized their true worth, the subjugators began to tremble. The poor lift themselves up in rebellion because the prophet has told them that they are destined to be free. When a people rise up and begin their march to freedom subjugation suddenly becomes repression, the hidden violence comes out in the open.

When Jesus announces the liberation of the people, he comes forward as a witness to a new kingdom. Then Pilate "washes his hands" because he has no need to sit in judgment; that thankless task is better left to the Sanhedrin or Herod. Herod represents the oligarchy of the dependent homeland. We thus have this arrangement: The empire (Pilate) is on top, then comes Herod and the Herodians, dominated by Rome but in turn dominating and exploiting the people. We see these three levels in operation at the time of the crucifixion. All Pilate has to do is wash his hands because he knows that the dependent oligarchy under him wishes the death of Jesus. It is the same as saying that a Latin American is going to take care of the death of the Brazilian priest Pereira Neto. The ones who kill him will act in the name of the dependent oligarchy which is exploiting the people in the name of those of the "center." It is really Herod, dependent on the center, who kills Jesus. Sin can do nothing else but kill life because, if life conquers, death dies. If Jesus, who is life, is allowed to live, the system, which is death, dies. Here precisely is the dialectic between death and life. Jesus dies as he must because repression brings about the disappearance of the witness to the kingdom to come.

The Violence of Sin

As long as the oppressed accept subjugation, sin (whether erotic, pedagogical, ideological, or political) is considered to be a natural fact, a sacred fact. There is no need, then, for any kind of violent repression. Subjugating violence needs no claws, like the lion who plays with the mouse. But when the oppressed people lift up their heads, with a will to freedom and love for the future, not hatred, war begins. In war not all are corrupt. Unjust indeed will be the army of the subjugators and just the army that defends itself in war and fights for liberation. San Martín and his grenadiers were violent, but just; he was a just liberator, a true hero. It is the "realists" who want to save the empire who wage unjust war, war in exactly its demonic sense. In war there are two sides: The one helps and defends the poor, the other wants to keep on subjugating them. The question of where sin is can be answered. Jesus accepts that the claws of sin's logic will tear him to pieces. Jesus witnesses to the future order. He does not kill anyone. The subjugators are the first to kill; and the first to die are the ones who witness to the future order—the martyrs, the prophets, the Christians.

The prophet has to become poor in order to hear the poor. Therefore Jesus is poor as a prophet, poor as one of the oppressed, and poor as exteriority. The poor person as the prophet of the eschatological poor acts on behalf of the oppressed poor to liberate them. Jesus is identified with the poor, and, listening to the poor who ask a new kingdom of him, he acts on behalf of those poor. In doing so, he subverts the established order. Therefore the order kills him.

Of the three meanings of the word "poor," the strongest is that of prophet, the poor according to the Spirit, consecrated by the Spirit. These are not the poor "in spirit," for whom it is acceptable to be subjugators or rich because their "hearts" are poor. These are subterfuges we use that allow us to align ourselves with the "prince of this world." The poor according to the Spirit are the servants of Yahweh and commit themselves historically, pedagogically, and economically. They are poor according to the Spirit, according to the otherness of the system. The Spirit is God, who comes to us if we are open, and stays away if we remain closed. We are never spiritual by nature; if we are spiritual, it is because the Spirit is within us, as St. Paul teaches.

Jesus is the poor man; Jesus is the martyr because he witnesses to the future kingdom; Jesus is the prophet because he speaks to the system and says, "Cursed be you

Pharisees! . . . Give to Caesar what is Caesar's." What? Money, of course. "Give to God what is God's." What? Adoration. Caesar is a mortal, he is not God; but to say that he is not is a sacrilege against the empire. This man is dangerous because he is witnessing to the subversion of the empire. For this reason "he died *under* Pontius Pilate."

I have read many commentaries on the creed. The latest I have seen is that of Karl Barth. Commenting on the words "he died under Pontius Pilate," the exegete puts himself in the place of Jesus, as do all the others. He considers the sufferings of Jesus, his resistance to them, but he fails to look from the other side—Who is killing Jesus? Why? What is his motivation? On learning that Jesus was to be killed, the apostles said, "No, this can't be!" But Jesus said, "We are going up to Jerusalem!" Because Jesus sees that "they" are closing in on him, the only solution is either to betray his mission or to die. "We are going up to Jerusalem."

There are moments in our life when we are not aware of being on the road to Jerusalem, but if we do not go to Jerusalem, we betray our faith. It happens at times that our Jerusalems are of minor consequence. Still the moment can come when our Jerusalem would be that of the Lord. We have already undergone much in Latin America and the same may well be in store for us many times over. It is hard to remain a Christian under torture, but we must be prepared for this. In Brazil nuns are being tortured because they want a more just order. Since the present order is "sacred," they are being killed in the name of the order.

This means that, for witnessing to the eschatological kingdom, Jesus, the Life of life, dies in the claws of death. "He died under Pontius Pilate." The same is happening today also; but only the great saints are capable of displaying clearly their opposition to the system even though they know they will be ground up by it. We stand in awe of their sanctity, their heroism, their spiritual struggles; but we tend to overlook the meaning of their challenge to their times. When Don Bosco rounded up all those orphans and gave them an education, the industrialists of Turin and northern Italy tipped their hand when they said, "This priest is going too far; he's becoming a bother." He was giving dignity to a poor people; but when those technical schools were taken over by influential urban groups, their prophetic contribution came to an end.

The Ethos of Liberation

In the praxis of liberation there are liberating virtues. First among them is the love of justice; it is the love of the Other as other—*charity*. Justice means giving to all people what is due them. But to give to the Other what is due them as other, and not as part of an unjust system, I must love them as other. Thus only in loving the Other as other will I go on to give them their due as persons and not as part of the system.

I cannot love people effectively as other if I do not *trust* their word. They cry out to me, "I'm hungry!" I answer, "Bums, you're hungry because you won't work." Since they shall make no further appeal to me, I have denied them as other. To trust is to have faith in the other; it means accepting their word out of a concrete praxis of commitment—this is the meaning of St. Thomas's *ex voluntate*. My intellect accepts what they say because they say it, even though I do not understand what they say.

The third position is *hope*. Hope means desiring that those who have appealed to me and told me of their hunger achieve their liberation, because I love them as other, that is, I "hope" they will no longer be hungry. These three fundamental positions—to love the Other as other, to believe their word, and to hope for their liberation, their salvation—these are the three alterative or theological virtues. The rest are subordinate.

Prudence knows how to listen to the voice of the Other; it knows how to orchestrate tactically its service. *Justice* is not merely the offer of bread but of more just laws; it could mean risking one's life so that one day there might be a more just order. Prudence and justice come into play in planning for the liberation of the poor. Anger, too, is involved, which is a manifestation of the virtue of *fortitude*. Being valiant is the capacity to commit oneself to the point of death, and this is the most difficult of all. To do so one must be poor. *Poverty* is an attitude. Poverty is not a question of having nothing but of a willingness to give up one's life for the poor. If I give up all my goods and join twenty people who have nothing, I will frequently have more than I had before: This is wealth and not poverty. The individual poverty of the monk many times comes to be wealth among many; it is security for the future.

The strength of Jesus evidenced itself when he pardoned those who were torturing him. He looked upon them as persons. He who did the nailing looked upon him as a mere thing, and not a person. But Jesus looked at *him* as a person, face-to-face, and forgave his torturer—the noblest act a person is capable of. A school teacher in Argentina just a few years ago was able to forgive the police who were torturing her with electric shock treatments. When we know that the torturer is not sin but only the instrument of sin, we win out over death by treating him or her as a person.

But bravery and fortitude are not enough; we need *temperance* also. Today the opposite of temperance is comfort, or socially acceptable pleasure. People today sell their lives in order not to lose their comfort. They watch what they say or do for fear of losing their jobs, and therefore no one is afraid of them. But those who have no fear of losing all they have bear watching. There is no point in telling Jesus that "we are going to take everything from you" when he had not even a place to lay his head. Jesus was unencumbered by things; he was poor and had no fear of losing anything. So there was no way to shut him up. He was a man to be feared. The only way to shut him up was to kill him. And this is precisely what they did.

Thus the *ethos* of liberation is all the virtues put to the service of liberation.

More About Violence

The violence that killed Jesus was the violence of the conquistador, repressive violence designed to nullify the authentic gesture of liberation. There is, on the other hand, the liberating violence of the liberator, for example, San Martín and his army of the Andes. Furthermore, there is the pedagogical violence of the prophet, the kind we see in Jesus. He organized a church and not a state. The function of the church will always be that of pedagogue and prophet, and not one of armed violence, not even in the cause of liberation. As a prophetic institution its function is eschatological—preaching what is to come. It takes a critical look at the fixation and anti-historicity of the totalized system, which is sin. The system would have wished that the Word of God had never come to this world. Nothing arouses greater anger in it than that God would have become man and placed himself *within* the system. Jesus Christ is now present until the end of time, continuously supplying Christians with the vocation of commitment to the poor. Having done away with the old order, these Christians work toward a new order. But they will have to do this over and over again. The function of the Christian is to deinstitutionalize the institutions of sin and, like Jesus in his identification with the poor, turn history toward eschatology.

"Being-in-the-Money"

At one point in their history people said that being rich was all that mattered. Then the Christians came along and said that people have a natural right to private property. And this is true if we are talking about what a person needs according to individual human nature: a car, a house, clothing, food. But a piece of land measuring a thousand square miles cannot be *natural* private property, but only juridically so. That kind of property has a social function. If I am able to make institutions work for the good of the poor, I am complying with the demands of the gospel. Excessive private property leads to an economic system of subjugation. In the time of the monarchy there were Christians who fought for democracy and they made out badly. Now, in a time of capitalist democracy and private enterprise, there are Christians who are fighting for a more perfect society that would be socialized. They are faring badly, too. It frequently happens also that the church aligns itself with the subjugators, and this is its sin. Only by identifying itself with the poor can the church liberate the world from an unjust system.

Natural private property is not contrary to socialistic principles because I have a natural right to whatever I need to live—things like calories, protein, clothing, housing, etc. There is no socialist system that quarrels with this. But the excessive and unjust accumulation of juridical private property is an offshoot of original sin, of the death of Abel, of the disobedience of Adam. It is at the root of the subjugation of peoples in Latin America.

If Jesus had respected the law, the Jewish "constitution" of the Sanhedrin, the reigning order and the socially acceptable virtues, he would have died an old man within the confines of the city. But he died *outside* the city—crucified.

On Palm Sunday the people celebrated the arrival of their king; the poor were quick to recognize his kingship. One week later, the great ones, the subjugators killed him. Jesus is the proclamation of the Parousia and the only ones who see him as king are the poor because he is one of them. The frenzy of Palm Sunday is the last straw; "he" will have to be killed because of the ugly situation brewing—*the people are following him.* His death a week later is a foregone conclusion.

His resurrection is the re-creation, the birth of the new person; it is death that has died and that which is born is new life, a new order. It is the new order that rises up unmerited in Christian history, a bonanza, the walking again of the paralytic. Jesus said, "You believe; well then, walk." The Christian today in Latin America says, "You, do you believe in Christ?" The other answers, "We'll wait and see." The prophets must risk themselves for the liberation of Latin America. It will believe if the paralytics walk again, if the people become free. Only in this way can we today give meaning to the kingdom of heaven.

We can no longer say, "We have no use for economics or politics; we believe only in the kingdom and nothing else because we reckon only with things of the spirit." What we would be doing in this instance, without realizing it, would be to consecrate the order, sin. Others can say, "We are betting everything on the historical kingdom." They do so with such enthusiasm that history becomes a new religion. When the new order takes over, the poor end up being subjugated all over again and we have a new divinization of the order.

Christians, however, assert that there is an eschatological order and a historical order; working toward the historical future which they know is not absolute, they witness to the eschatological kingdom. The doctrine of the Incarnation allows us to say that we have to commit ourselves to a historical, pedagogical, political level, but only as a sign of the eschatological.

This is so very obvious, yet how often are there misunderstandings! How often do people say, "Watch out for Latin American messianism!" Messianism in the temporal order that becomes absolutized is bad; but if we temper it with a view to the eschatological, it is perfect. If we do nothing more than cry out against messianism in the temporal order, we eviscerate the Christian's critical contribution; we put ourselves on the side of the prevailing order and we make Christianity the opium of the people.

If we say, "Bear with your suffering because the king will come!" we are saying, "Accept the Devil!" In this case the kingdom of God will not come; the kingdom to come will be the kingdom of this world.

It is wrong to preach "resignation." On the contrary, we should preach a holy liberating Christian restlessness for the coming of the kingdom. Be resigned, yes, when it comes our turn to shoulder the cross. But in an active way. In the moment of our inevitable crucifixion, we shall have to resign ourselves. There is a difference.

3

The Theology of Politics: Toward a Latin American Ecclesiology

> *I believe . . . in the Holy Spirit,
> in the Holy Church.*
>
> Apostles' Creed

In the previous chapters we gave an example of the possibility of discourse, a way of thinking. Using certain categories, we have restated the question of ethics, what I could have called moral theology but which, in reality, is simply a branch of the one theology in praxis.

In this chapter I would like to dwell on the following theme: a Latin American ecclesiology. Here I will deal with another article of the creed: "I believe in the Holy Spirit, in the Holy Church"; this is how the most ancient of creeds states it (Denzinger, 1963; no. 11). I intend to go into the theology of politics. The question we should ask ourselves is: What is the function of the church in world history? Or, more simply: What is the function of the church? You realize that we are in a crisis, a very difficult situation because some, seeing that the church is not responsive to certain demands, leave the church. Others, perhaps, demand of the church works and functions that are not its task. For this reason, I believe that the church is in the center of all our discussions. On previous occasions I have pointed out that to deal with the history of the church is to deal with ecclesiology. I want to treat this theme in more depth.

Preliminary Clarifications

I believe that theological discourse should always begin with a theologal anthropology, that is, with people, because God revealed himself to people. Even what we can say of God in himself is what has been revealed to us; it has been revealed to people as people are. This means that theology has to be anthropological. But this anthropology has distinct levels, and I would like now to take time to talk about these levels in order to have a better understanding of what is meant by the theology of politics, an ecclesiology.

We have seen that the fundamental categories we were using relate to the confrontation between what we called *totality*—which at base is always "my world," since it always begins with the self—and the otherness that is beyond the self. Moses is an example of the self to whom God spoke. Here we can use the very same categories. We always start with a world; but in Judeo-Christian thinking the world we start with is always secondary. The Other is always felt to be primary, as the origin. Here precisely is the difference between Greek and Hegelian (by that I mean modern European) thought and Judeo-Christian thought.

The Christian does not begin with the self but with the Other, whether it be the father, the mother, the homeland, or history, or, lastly, God the Creator. The whole idea of creation indicates precisely that before the self there is an Other. The confrontation that I spoke of is the face-to-face stance. It is said of Moses that he was "face-to-face with God."

"Face-to-face" is the experience of someone before an Other recognized as someone. Let me give a simple example. You arrive at an institution and are met by a person who is nothing more than an employee to you. You do not recognize him as "someone" but as just an adjunct of the institution. But if this person suddenly turns out to be an old friend, you say, "Hi, John, how are you?" He ceases to be an employee and becomes someone that we are asking something of. You expect his answer to be informative; otherwise you would not have asked your question. Someone facing someone and putting a question to that person—this has to be an interpersonal experience.

For me to come face-to-face with someone—the Other—I have to see that person as free and not just a thing in my world that I could dominate. If I am a boss, I can dominate the worker. But if I see the worker as "someone," then he or she is much more than just a cog in the wheel; that worker becomes a mystery standing before me, as exteriority, as someone who is beyond the system I rule over. The system can be my home, my factory, my neighborhood—my world. We have already noted that the word "world" means "flesh." Christ uses the word to mean "totality." The Other as free is always going to be beyond the world, my world, my totality. The experience of the face-to-face is proper to the Semite tradition (it is found in the Code of Hammurabi) but it is also part of the Hebrew tradition as expressed in the thinking of the prophets. Later on Christ will equate it to the kingdom of heaven.

The face-to-face is not to be confused with "vision." Vision always occurs within a world (I *see* things, I *know* them). But I do not see the Other as other; I love and respect the Other as other and I ask who he or she is. The Other is beyond my vision, in the realm of justice and love. This experience of the face-to-face is proper to and basic to all Judeo-Christian thinking.

"Face" means countenance and countenance is the person. It is precisely here that the formulation of trinitarian dogma began. God reveals himself to humankind (who is also a countenance) in three ways: as the Father-Creator, as the Son-Word that is incarnated, or as Spirit. These three countenances or persons of God are what I would now like to talk about. But keep in mind that these three countenances belong to the Other, not to me, in the sense that, at heart, I will never see or experience *my* countenance.

The Erotic, Pedagogical, and Political Relationships

This experience of face-to-face may seem abstract, but it is really concrete. Someone's countenance comes face-to-face with the countenance of a concrete other.

The first manner of self-revelation to others I will call the erotic. The Song of Songs comes to mind: "Kiss me with the kiss of your mouth." The book is about the relationship between a man and a woman. I call it erotic in the sense that the first face-to-face is that of a man with a woman. Of course, the Song of Songs is not only about a couple; it also sings of the unity of the church or of the world with God its Creator.

We are dealing here with a theological eroticism in which the face-to-face becomes mouth-to-mouth and, by a further extension of Hebrew thought, sexual intercourse. All other relationships, even the political, have their basis in this erotic relationship.

In the man-woman relationship there can be either respect for the Other or domination of the Other—the sin of domination. This happens when the woman, who is the Other in the world of eroticism, is not respected as other but is used as a thing, a sex object, housewife, nursemaid to children, doer of multiple household tasks. Woman, nothing more than a thing, has been at the disposal of man for thousands of years; it just happens that Indo-European and Semite thought has always called God the Father.

In reality, as Paul Ricoeur has well noted, the title "Father" that we give to God is nothing more than a symbol, a symbol that designates him as the creative origin of all things. But because of male dominance, we stick with the word "father." The male dominates our world even in the purest and most perfect symbolic language.

When the female ceases to be Other to the male, the totality is dominated by the male. This gives rise to the first sin: the subjugation of woman. How is the liberation of woman to be achieved? We said that ethics studied the nature of liberation and it proved to be a matter of the "center" and of the "periphery." But this is political liberation on an international scale. Woman's liberation begins by being, first and foremost, erotic liberation, which entails the woman's moving from the status of alienation to being the Other to the male—a face-to-face relationship between two free people.

If we were to take a whole new look at this question, we would see that sin, subjugation, has made of *the home* (this is the world of the erotic) a totality where the woman is locked up in a kind of prison. The man goes freely out the door to work while the woman stays in seclusion. We have not yet got around to a theology of the married couple. We have taken a few steps in that direction but we are only just beginning. We need to scrap all our notions about the erotic act and start over again if we are ever really going to bring about women's liberation.

The man-woman relationship will be normal and liberated only when one free person stands before the other who is also free. Only then will we see the fullness of *eros*. But what in fact happens? Even when two people who are free enter a marriage, both can end being totalized all over again and killing the Other. The *new* other that can be killed is a third party—the child. Its life can be snuffed out by abortion or it can be brought up along the same lines as the parents. I would call this the pedagogy of subjugation. The child will not become a fresh, new being but an echo of the parents. Basically they will teach it to be what they are. The child will not be a new, messianic, anointed chapter of history; in one sense it will be killed off.

The child then, growing up under the totalized couple, even in the best of care becomes once more the alienated one, dominated by the father and the mother. Given that the child is allowed to be born, it is subjected to educational dominance. We call this second phase of the parent-child, teacher-pupil relationship "pedagogy."

Remember that Jesus was not called "father," nor "mother" either, naturally. He was called above all "teacher"—"rabbi." This means that Jesus established with his disciples (and the church in turn does the same with the world) a pedagogical relationship which in reality was prophetic. Thus we are no longer on the erotic level but have come to the pedagogical level.

If the child is brought up in the exact model of the parents, we are faced with a case of pedagogical subjugation. This is to a great extent the source of rebelliousness of the young; they become aware that they are expected to walk the same road as adults. The demand "to be like people have always been" brings on a kind of alienation.

Liberating the child is the same as pedagogical liberation. The relationship of parent-child or teacher-pupil must become a matter of respecting the child as Other and showing it the way in which it can arrive at being a free person in the presence of the free. In essence, this is the problem of pedagogical liberation.

Only when the child becomes a free being in the presence of a free being (the parent or the teacher) will the two become colleagues. When the teacher is able to hammer home to the pupil that he or she is equal to the teacher, they become colleagues. When the parent is able to lead the child gently toward adulthood, they become "brothers." And, precisely, the relationship between one brother and another is the third relationship that I call "political." It is a relationship of brothers as equals. It is perhaps on this level that the most frightening kind of alienation takes place repeatedly. When a brother does not respect another brother, he or she places the other one in subjugation—the domination of brother over brother or of master over slave. In humankind's history there have been many inequities and subjugations, including the latest of the center over the periphery—widespread political subjugations of brother over brother.

Even on this level of political subjugation—the last of the three—political liberation will happen and the subjugated brother will come to be equal to the free person and will live in justice. This political liberation is the third phase. The political subjugator conditions the erotic subjugator, and the latter the pedagogical, and the pedagogical the political, and vice versa, in such a way that it is impossible to determine which is metaphysically first.

In the erotic relationship the woman learns, in her domestic upbringing, that she is to be the servant of the male. From early childhood she is told that "girls play with dolls and boys learn to fight." Her education is directed toward being the servant, whereas he is trained to subjugate the world. This is also, and in the last analysis, a political question. She in turn trains her daughter to be the slave of her future husband and her son to be the lord and master that she never was. When we train the son to be subjugator, we are laying the groundwork for political behavior. But we could just as well begin our analysis with the political and it would be altogether proper to see the politico-economic as paramount and the other phases conditioned by it. At any rate, all these problems can be stated theologically because Christ is related to them all.

Our God reveals himself as Father and as Teacher, Son and Brother. All this has to do with Christian thinking. Besides being real, it is also theological, as we learn from the Old and New Testaments. They are categories that should stimulate our thinking.

To conclude, ecclesiology is the theology that deals with the political aspect of theology. We need to know how to explain the prophetic-pedagogical function of the church in the political history of the world.

Ecclesiology as Politics and Pedagogy

Our question was: What function does the church perform? What is the church for? The answer will come to us in part through theological reflection—the study of the relationship between brothers insofar as they are Christians. The relationship of one Christian with another within the ecclesial body is a matter of politics, because it is a relationship among the parts of a whole. But the church's role in the world is pedagogical. This is not the same thing as a political role, because the church is not a state. The state takes care of the political side of things whereas the church, being a community of brothers (theologal politics), fulfills a pedagogical, prophetic role. For this reason I repeat: Ecclesiology considers theologal politics as a relationship of brothers within the ecclesial community, but with regard to *prophetico-pedagogical function* in world history.

So the question remains: What is the function of the church? Better still, what in fact has the church accomplished up till now in world history and, more concretely, in Latin America? We might answer, Nothing! If this would be our answer, we would be at a loss to know what is our function at the present moment.

The Greek word for church is *ekklesía,* meaning "the assembly of those called together"; the Hebrew word is *kahal,* meaning "to summon the people," "those brought together for." The question then arises: Brought together for *what?* This is the vital question. To put it another way: What role should the church play in the process of universal liberation, specifically in Latin America? The answer should make clear to what degree the church at times fails, sins, for not having taken the stand it should have in the process, maintaining an unshakable status quo or perhaps aligning itself on the side of sin. Before answering the question, we ought to take a clear look at other considerations.

Ecclesial Prehistory and Protohistory

To understand the church, we have to begin with its prehistory, the history of the non-Christian world—what we usually call the pagan world. In reality, though, the pre-Christian world was nothing more than the "flesh," the totality before the coming of the Word. The Hebrews went *into* Canaan, a pre-Israelite world. The Christians went *into* the Roman empire, a pre-Christian world. Christians came to America and discovered there the Aztecs, the Tupi Guarani, the Caribs, the Incas—a pre-Christian world. Why is there always this kind of confrontation? Because it is of the nature of the church to insert itself. First there is a totality which does not yet have that which will come to it. This is the prehistory of salvation.

Afterward, there is a protohistory of the church. Israel—and we keep coming back to it—is its protohistory. Israel has a very interesting structure and I would like to talk about several aspects of it. First, there is the faith of Abraham. In Hebrews 11 we read: "Abraham believed." (There is a similarity here between the faith of Abraham and the openness of the Virgin Mary to the Spirit.) Abraham lived *in* the totality that was pre-Hebrew and even pre-revelation. He was just one more citizen in the third dynasty of Ur. He heard the Word and the Word offered a covenant to him. Think about it—in a pre-covenant world, someone speaks to him and he believes, he believes the Word of the Other and, accepting it to be true, he journeys forth on the strength of the word of the Other, with no guarantee other than that the Other had spoken to him. This is faith. There is a whole anthropological structure to faith: Abraham believed in someone, the Other; he took this word to be true; acceptance led to commitment because he left his homeland and journeyed through strange lands. This is precisely a process of liberation because he went from Ur of the Chaldees to the promised land, solely on the word of the Other and before the time of Moses.

This structure of Abraham's faith is at the heart of what will come later.

Abraham ratified the covenant, affirming his belief that God would look favorably on all who believed as he did, those who would reject the totality and be capable of opening themselves to the Other, risking themselves for the Other. Concretely, the Other is always the poor, because they are beyond any possible system of exploitation. It was because of the covenant that a small tribe began its history of wandering as foreigners. Foreignness is a must for leaving totality behind and setting out for uncharted lands.

But the foreignness of the clan was transformed much later into a monarchy. With this transformation they were once more locked into totality. This is why Samuel, a prophet who leads a nomadic existence, wants to do away with every possible monarchic or political system. When the Israelites express a desire for a monarchy, Samuel asks them: Have you thought about how dangerous it is to have a king (1 Sam. 8–10)? Kings subjugate people. The prophet does not want to anoint a king because to anoint a king is to bring about totality. This will have a great deal of importance in later history. But they went ahead and anointed a king—Saul. From that moment there began the dialectic between the king and the prophet who spoke in the name of the Lord. The dialectic will continue for the duration of the monarchy. But what happens after this?

Upon the disappearance of the kingdom of Israel, the Israelites become foreigners, first in the Babylonian world, later in the Greek world and, finally, in the Roman world. It is the time of the diaspora. They cease being an ethnic and monarchic kingdom and become a *religious* community. It is worthy of note that the Jews can continue to be a religious community without any political backing.

This experience of the Hebrew world is transmitted to Christianity. The Jews discovered that any conceivable empire is not the kingdom of heaven, in a way that enabled them to wait for the kingdom, the coming of the Messiah, without the backing of a formal government. This is the great experience of the diaspora as far as its proselytes were concerned. Remember that Paul would use the experience of the Jews in his preaching of the gospel of Jesus, starting in the synagogues. Without this first experience, the second would have been impossible. Therefore, the church will never be a political state like the monarchy of Israel. It learned from Israel's experience to be a diaspora or an eschatological religious community. At any rate the Jews had also an *institution* in the diaspora—the synagogue. The synagogue had a definite structure as an institution. But it was pedagogical and not political, because in the synagogue there was no assumption or exercise of power. Its function was to teach the Law. The pagan proselyte was educated in the Law. This means that the Jews saw a clear distinction between the political community of the monarchy and the religious community of the synagogue with its prophetic or eschatological sense. So it is very easy to demonstrate the importance of this process.

Properly speaking, the history of the church begins with the fact of Christ who is the culmination of the vocation of Israel's "remnant." Jesus will not start from scratch but will build on the experience of Israel. He will not structure a temporal kingdom and, therefore, when the Zealots want to consecrate him king, which is the same as trying to make him a political candidate, Jesus says No to this. But behind this No is his eschatological strategy and his historical tactic. We have to take a keen look at the question. The church has its beginning in Jesus, the Teacher, and his disciples; there is a pedagogical relationship here—the rabbi and the Twelve. Those Twelve constituted a small community. That first community will later be extended to Samaria; it will go to

Antioch where it will have its first Hellenistic experience. The Corinthian community will be made up of people who were nothing more than pagans.

Then comes the great story of the persecutions. Why did the Christians die? Why did Jesus die under Pontius Pilate? For the same reasons that Christians were persecuted under the Roman empire—Rome had divinized, made a god of, the emperor. Christians lived within the empire but among the poorest of the poor. They dwelt among the lower, but not necessarily the vulgar, classes. In their poverty, the Christians had no great estates, or the huge armies of the empire, or the proud fleets that sailed the Mediterranean. But in their poverty they proclaimed the eschatological kingdom and thus called into question the divinity of the emperor and the system of the empire. With their vision of, and hope for, the rebirth of humankind, they became the target for the lances of the emperor. They were dragged to the arena as atheists. The Christians, atheists in regard to the emperor, were a subversive threat to the reigning kingdom. In a sense the Christians—awaiting a future kingdom—were responsible for what was later to be the Holy Roman empire or the Byzantine empire. They did not fight for this later historic development but they certainly sowed the seeds for it. They were really battling for another, eschatological kingdom. At any rate they became the moving force of history, detotalizing the Roman empire and casting it in a whole new mold.

The First Cultural Totalization of Christianity

The Christians themselves became a new totality called Christendom—the Holy Roman empire or the Byzantine empire. Christendom got its start toward totalization from a twisted understanding of Augustine's concept of the city of God. The city of God and the city of the Devil were precisely two cities, the former of otherness and the latter of totality. Augustine says that those who love themselves are the founders of the Devil's city, whereas those who love God, that is, the Other, constitute the kingdom of heaven. But medieval people juggled Augustine's concept around and said, "Roman or Byzantine Christendom is the kingdom of God and the Arabs are the infidels." They thereby made a culture out of the kingdom of God and totalized this culture. Totalization means the identification of the church with the temporal state or the culture. All totalization is sin. The church, upon becoming totalized, loses its critical exteriority and puts itself forward as an institution *in* which all are to be saved. Herein arises the theology of Christendom, a theology of the Eucharist, of baptism, of the church, of the whole.

Clearly, then, if everything is taken care of and we are already in the kingdom of heaven and the feudal lords along with the princes and kings are the depositories of the authority of God, we can baptize everybody practically at the moment of birth. The church as an institution is part of Christendom and in turn sees the order as sacred. Whoever rebels against the feudal lord rebels not only against the natural law but also against the divine law. There thus comes a point where exteriority is identified with totality because there is only the one order. This is why a theologian from Uruguay says that "in Christendom there is no mission because everybody is Christian." If there is no mission, there is no prophecy. And if there is no prophecy, all we have is an ecclesiastical institution identified with the culture. If this is so, we are then in a situation of sin because the church has become totalized.

And how are the non-Christians treated? They are

turned over to the secular arm and burned at the stake. The other is murdered: Stalin's Siberia and the jails of the Inquisition are methods for erasing the other. In both instances the same logic is at work. The other, instead of being loved and respected, is murdered and therefore the totality is totalized; it becomes impossible to break out of it and go beyond it. This theology of Christendom, this identification of the church with a given culture, is part of the crisis we are suffering from. The big problem lies in getting beyond the crisis.

First Thesis: The Church "Before" the World

In the first place, the church is always and primarily *before* the world. Thus, if there is totality in the pre-Christian world, if the world is already a given, already created, it will now be re-created, reborn through the function of the church. We begin with a world constituted as created. The church nevertheless comes from outside and as already preconstituted. The first position of the church is to invade the world from outside. It can also be said that this is its first function: The church is a "face-to-face" of itself with the world. This face-to-face, which every Christian lives out on an individual level and which is lived out also on the social and even historico-political level, signifies crisis—in the Greek sense, from the verb *krinein*, which means "to be critical," "to separate." To criticize means to stand at a distance in order to form a judgment. This criterion or judgment is, in a way, the "judgment of God." It is revealed to us, or, better still, we discover what is the meaning of totality as totality. The multitude that dwelt in the Holy Roman empire, or in Hispanic Christendom, or wherever, accepted totality as divine, as totally obvious. They were completely naive in regard to totality as such. They exclaimed: "Our kingdom is the only one blessed by God and apart from it there is nothing but barbarism." If we lived in barbarism, we would see that it is not so barbarous and that it makes its own kind of sense.

Where there is no "separation," no standing at a distance, there is no crisis. The one who comes from outside criticizes totality as totality and finds it totalized. This is why the early Christians were able to see that the Roman empire was demoniacal. Were they exaggerating? By no means, because when the Romans proclaimed the empire and the emperor to be divine, they were totalizing the whole system. But the same thing happens in our "Western and Christian" civilization: If we totalize it uncritically we also end with a demoniacal totality.

In the first place, then, occurs the crisis, in such a way that the church, the Spirit, comes from out of exteriority. The Spirit is *in* the church and that Spirit invades the world as Word. But that Word is a prophetic word, critical of totalization. If the church does not issue a summons to the world, if it does not point out to the world that it has closed in upon itself, it has failed in its essential mission. Its first step should be to criticize. This is where the dialectic begins between the king and the prophet, between Moses and the pharaoh, between Jesus and the leaders of his people—not to mention present-day instances.

The great epochs of the church occurred when the church exercised its critico-prophetic function, not just in calling attention to the sinful totalization of a system but also at the same time in pointing the way to liberation, a way out of totalization. To be concrete, how was all this set forth in Latin America? First there was totality that was the Amerindian world. It was made up of Aztecs, Incas, Caribs, who heard the prophetic voice of very few missionaries. Bartolomé de las Casas, for example, makes a clear distinction between conquest and evangelization. Conquest is the precise opposite of evangelization because conquerors do not respect the other who is merely a thing in their world, whereas the evangelist respects the world and the culture of the other and liberates the other from self. This is what Paulo Freire calls the pedagogy of the oppressed.

This first Amerindian totality becomes partly evangelized but very soon the Word is stifled by a world become totalized all over again. Indians were gathered into Hispanic Christendom only to find themselves in a new kind of totalization where they cannot be Christian and Indian but are Christian and exploited workers in the viceroyship of Peru. Indians are stripped of their human dignity and become aliens in a culture where the evangelizing Word often serves no other purpose but that of integrating them, after baptism, into a civilization that exploits them. We have the word of many missionaries for this. To what end did we evangelize the Indian man who sold fish in Asunción for a living or the Indian woman who did domestic chores, sleeping with the master and fulfilling other functions even more degrading? Just how far did the Word penetrate this world after the sixteenth century?

Jesus talks explicitly about this Word in the parable of the Sower. God, through the church, sows seed that falls in different kinds of soil. Hence let there be an analogous acceptance of it.

Our first thesis, then: The church prophesies from the outside.

Second Thesis: The Church "in" the World

The church is not only "before" the world but also "in" it. You will remember the alternative of which Jesus spoke: "I do not ask that you take them out of the world but that you preserve them from the Evil One." The church invades, enters *into* the world.

The church is not made up of only the oppressed even though Christ came among us and took the form of a servant. The church is also human and takes on not only the form of a slave but often the form of the oppressor. This becomes a very serious matter. Because the church is *in* the world, it assumes the errors of the world. There are Christians who are poor by choice or because of an accident of birth. On the other hand, there are Christian subjugators who collaborate with the sin of subjugation—the only sin. The Christians who identify with the powerful, the rich, the elite, the oppressors tend to divinize the reigning system. They are the ones who "consecrate" the historic states and defend the power of kings, emperors, lords, and presidents as a matter of divine delegation. In essence the system becomes divinized and prophecy is out of the question. Christians who identify with the poor, on the other hand, are free in the face of the system. Having nothing, they have nothing to lose and nothing to defend in the system. Poverty as an evangelical disposition is nothing more than an openness to the future, to the eschatological kingdom; it stands free before the temporal kingdom, the reigning totality. Only when the church identifies itself with the poor and the oppressed can it accomplish its prophetic function.

When Christians identified themselves with the powerful after having suffered persecution for their defense of the poor in the Roman empire, they adopted as their own the culture of the empire. It was thus that they adopted the pagan Latin language, which came to be considered sacred. What a chore it was to rid ourselves of Latin! A pagan tongue and we took it to be the most sacred of languages.

The process of incarnation, in-totalization is difficult

but, once it is accomplished, it is not easy to free the church from it. This enfleshment of the Word is a process of acculturation in which Christians absorb a culture. It is a happening that apologists have to contend with. They attempt to preach the gospel to the Romans, using Roman categories. In the *Letter to Diognetus* it says that in nothing do we Christians differ from the Romans; we dress the same, speak and write the same language, and do the same kind of work. There is only the difference that we Christians adore a God who is not a creature. How deeply the Christian became assimilated to the Roman empire! And this is what distinguished the Christians from the Jews. The Jews remained "separated" (*farisim:* Pharisees) because they had a vocation to prophecy, but they did not accept the Incarnation.

The Jews lack the Incarnation and this is where we Christians have differed from all Jews at all times. They have never had a sense of incarnation.

In Latin America (Amerindia) the evangelization entered into a culture and, at the same time, became a Christendom. This incarnation in the form of colonial Christendom supposes, nevertheless, the assumption of all the errors of totality. This totality, as we have said, has a center and a periphery. The peripheral world in turn has an elite and a people. And indeed the church is in the "center" (in France, the United States, and, in the case of the Byzantine church, in Russia); it is found in our oligarchies, naturally, in our upper classes, and also in the oppressed. We have here a strangely equivocal situation. Every sociological analysis of dependence or of social classes ought to be taken into account here and put to use. The church is *real* but it is also equivocal as far as its concrete manifestation is concerned.

There are subjugators and subjugated in the church and no ecclesiology can afford to overlook this fact. But that brings up the question: How accommodating can the church be? Are the ones who collaborate with subjugation as "angels" of the "prince of this world" really a part of the church? If we say No, then we will have to let them know that they are not Christians. This is a serious matter.

The parable of the Wheat and the Chaff sheds light on this problem. It is not up to us to root out the non-Christian elements in the church, because we are not the "judgment of God." But it is certainly not the same thing to be poor among the subjugated as it is to be influential among the subjugators, because the subjugators commit sin and cause scandal, whereas the poor do not commit the sin of subjugation but are, rather, the victims of it. The poor person is the just person. For this reason Jesus chose to be poor, a "man of the people." It does matter what side we are on. The church, living *in* the concrete reality, falls into the equivocacy of the world. When this goes unnoticed, an aristocracy that calls itself Christian will want to manipulate the church. The most genuine thing about the church, that which is Christ in it, is the poor, not because they are poor but because, being dominated by the system, the poor are at the same time *exterior* to it. An example would be a poor man going by a rich man's house on a cold winter's day. Shivering with the cold, he sees the rich man through the window basking in the warmth of an open fire. There are two different worlds—and the poor man is outside the rich man's world.

The poor are always on the outside. They go to the bank to ask for a loan, but, because they have no assets, they come away empty-handed. The rich man, on the other hand, who already has millions, is given more millions. Or take the case of the poor woman going to the Post Office to buy stamps; she must wait at the end of the line. But a lawyer coming in goes right to the head of the line and says, "I'm in a big hurry." The poor woman, saying nothing, waits patiently for her turn. All day, everywhere, the poor are made to feel outside. They are unable to cope with the intricacies of the system. All they know how to do is put up with abuse. This *experience* of exteriority is at the root of the gospel saying, "theirs [the poor] is the kingdom of heaven." They are already in the kingdom because in the exteriority of the present system lies the future, the eschatological kingdom. This is not a question of symbolism but of concrete reality: "Blessed are the poor for theirs is the kingdom of heaven."

The Beatitudes were seen to be paradoxical (in Greek *paradoxon* is the opposite of a common opinion). Of course, the Beatitudes go against the opinion of the totality. But if we are able to perceive "the logic of exteriority," they become perfectly rational. The Beatitudes are to be taken in a very literal sense.

The church, then, is *in* the world—in its *in*carnation. But being enfleshed, it gets mixed up in the errors of history. Nevertheless it has criteria for discerning its function.

Third Thesis: The Church as Prophetic Institution

We can now begin to describe the nature of the church. The church is a prophetic institution. It is an institution but at the same time it is prophecy. It can be said that it is a new paradox. It certainly seems unthinkable that an institution could also be prophetic.

Let us use as an example a priest who would be completely perverse, whose only ambition is to become rich by using church money to invest in property. We would say that he has become totalized. Nevertheless he remains an institution. And so it is that he reads the gospel on a Sunday morning, which is heard by a young person who then feels called to prophecy. We have here a paradox, but the church is an institution that proclaims prophecy. If there were no institution, prophecy would be pure anarchy, a utopia without content.

If the institution had no prophecy, it would be annihilated, it would be totalized in sin. Latin Christendom, because it would not allow for exteriority, downgraded prophecy as a mission. It totalized the culture; the lord bishop had armies and was a temporal power. An example of this was the archbishop of Toledo before the reforms of Cisneros.

The church is a prophetic institution. When the institution closes in on itself, becomes totalized, as did Latin America's colonial Christendom, seeing Christ as "King" becomes most acceptable. To see him as "King" is appropriate for someone who is totalized. If, in my totalization, I do not look to the future, I begin to interpret the church from the point of view of the political state. I want Christendom with its princes and kings to be like the political state. Thus arises the figure of the king. "Christ the King" is a new name for Christ born of a certain totalization of the institution. What a far-fetched and ill-defined name for the Christ who historically did not want to be crowned king—although ironically they nailed to the cross the inscription JESUS OF NAZARETH, KING OF THE JEWS. Whenever totalization gets into trouble, people spring to its defense in the name of orthodoxy.

From 1930 on there had been growing among Latin Americans the ideal of a New Christendom. Catholic Action set out to reconvert Argentina and other nations of Latin America into Catholic nations. By "Catholic" was meant the Middle Ages and a great deal was said about that in the 1930s. Leon Bloy, Charles Péguy, and many others glorified the Middle Ages. The church was again identified with a culture. Since there was a crisis, the question was how to reintroduce the medieval totality or at least defend it. There was much talk about defending the faith ("secretariats for the defense of the faith" were very much the order of the day). And instead of undertaking the mission of exteriority, this was seen to be the enemy, because we were totalized and we were defending ourselves against the other. People defend themselves against the other when they are not in a state of mission or prophecy; in a state of totalization, mission is impossible and even more so when people think they must defend the institution as an absolute.

The intraecclesial defense of the church is a sin on the part of the church. It brings to mind the parable of the Leaven and the Dough. If the leaven is removed from the dough and is constituted as totality, it rots. It works as leaven only when it is inside the dough. It is leaven and nothing else. This means that there is an institution, but it makes sense only by doing the job of fermenting the dough. Apart from the dough, it rots.

Thus it was that Christendom was losing out in the defense of the faith. Faith needs no defense. How will I defend the faith if I see the other as an enemy? In whom will I believe if I have no one in whom to believe? The only thing I would then be defending would be a doctrine. But faith can never be reduced to a mere doctrine because faith is to accept the word of the other, of the poor who today are the epiphany of God. If the other is for me the infidel, the barbarian, the enemy against whom I am on the defensive, faith becomes impossible. I am in a totalization, which bars me from mission; this is sin.

The church, on the other hand, is essentially a missionary and prophetic institution and, as I will explain later, a liberating institution. I cannot first define the institution and then the mission, as we were once taught—organize the community first and then go forth to the apostolate; organize the community first and then figure in what way we are to be prophetic. No indeed! The community is to be organized *around* what we call apostolate, it is to be organized *in* and *for* prophecy, mission, and service to exteriority. If we start first with community only, the essential law of its constitution is already contradicted. At whatever point there is no exteriority for the church to fulfill its mission, it would die. And we shouldn't be at all surprised, when at the end of time the kingdom comes, that the church would disappear because it would no longer be necessary, because there would be no historic exteriority. The kingdom will have come.

We speak of the militant church and of the triumphant church. The triumphant church is not the militant church; it is the church that remains when the militant church disappears. What I mean is that when the church has no exteriority, it disappears. When it becomes totalized in the shape of Christendom and can no longer anticipate the kingdom of heaven, it passes itself off as the kingdom; and that puts us right at the portals of hell. To pretend that I rule heaven is to set myself up as a "prince of this world"; as an idol of a divinized system, I proclaim, "We are already in the kingdom of heaven."

It should be observed here just how intrinsic it is to the church to be defined in terms of exteriority and how its essence is at stake in this regard.

Let us use a concrete example. We still see among us the religiosity of the people. If we want to bring about an effective pastoral praxis among the people, we must first bring about reforms in the church. The clergy, for example, if they are trained apart from the day-to-day living of the people cannot undertake a real pastoral praxis among the people. If we are to have such a praxis, clerical recruitment and formation must be reformed.

This does not mean, however, that the reformation should come first and later the apostolate, but that in the act of prophesying to the world, we will find that we will have to reform ourselves. This is the exact opposite of what we so frequently hear. Hans Küng, the great German theologian, as well as almost all European theologians, considers the church *in itself (ad intra)*. It's what we call intraecclesial thinking. All they are doing is totalizing the church and never coming to the solution demanded, because to reform the church our thinking first has to revolve around the extraecclesial, whence the demands for internal reform will come.

Our theology has to be of the world, and from that world will come the demands of the poor for reform in the church, because the church is a *prophetic* institution. In the *institution* we find all that is historic, real, and concrete in the church. On the *prophetic* side we find all that is eschatological in it. We must not overlook either of the two dialectical extremes. Some are so concerned about the institution that they wish the prophets would clear out. The prophet is tempted at times into thinking, "Come what may, I shall fulfill *my* mission." But we should add that almost always they end up beating the air, in the sense that they get so involved in their own apostolate that they find themselves cut off from the institution, alone, in the camp of the enemy without a rear guard. In the end they fail to do whay they set out to do and have to fight just to stay alive.

Of course there are others who say, "Look at those crazy guys beating the air! I'll stay with the institution even if it doesn't get reformed," and they do nothing. This is not the right attitude either. To accept the church as it is is to betray the church in its very essence.

The hard task of the missionary, of the prophet, of the Christian is to be open to prophecy, maintaining a critical stance within the institution.

In Latin America, secularization—that is, the slow withdrawal of the world, because of its growing autonomy since the nineteenth century, from the church (in the sense that the world began taking land and money from the church and undermining its political and educational influence)—is liberating the church for its role of prophecy. Secularization is the "arm of the Gentiles" all over again, because the church had become identified with the colonial culture, with colonial Christendom.

As it becomes poor, the church is obliged to tilt toward exteriority; in doing so, it will pronounce the prophetic word. Poverty is the condition that makes prophecy possible. If I have property and money and they put pressure on me, saying, "You keep quiet or we will confiscate your property and everything you have in the bank," I will be tied hand and foot and will be incapable of the prophetic function. If, on the other hand, I have nothing in the bank, I cannot be the victim of extortion. Prophecy demands poverty. Poverty is not a virtue to be desired for itself, because in this case it would be meaningless. Poverty is the giving of one's life in the fulfillment of the prophetic role. Those who are in no way compromised to totality because of poverty, can, from their exteriority, confront totality with its sin; they can criticize.

Thus secularization, this withdrawal of the world from the church, this preventing the church from exercising power, is the opening of the way to prophecy. It is the parable about the light not made to be hidden. Jesus says that when the light is hidden under the basket, we have to be able to take it out, to bring it to exteriority. Exteriority speaks to us of Christ (Messiah, prophet, anointed) and no longer of the King. Christ the *King* is not the prophet of Galilee, the "suffering servant."

At the beginning of this chapter I put forth the article of the creed that reads, "I believe in the Holy Spirit, in the Holy Church." Holy is *only* "the Other." No one is ever holy, but only that which is to come. The Other is mystery, the one to be honored. Hence the church is holy when it preserves exteriority from every system, when it prophesies eschatologically against a totalized totality.

Prophetico-Pedagogical Function of the Church in the World

I can now go back to the question I asked at the beginning of this chapter: What is the function of the church? Only now can I answer in the following way: Its function is a prophetico-pedagogical function of liberation. I am using the word "liberation" in its traditional sense to indicate at the same time "salvation" and "redemption." But I am also using the word in its economic and political sense, to indicate liberation from economic dependence, pedagogical dependence, erotic dependence, etc. The advantage of the word "liberation" is that, taking it in its biblical sense but also in its concrete and socio-political sense, it is charged with a strength that the word "salvation" no longer has. Salvation has an ethereal sense and has become almost meaningless. That is why I say that the church's function is a prophetico-pedagogical function of liberation.

Again, this means that history, in its economic, political, and pedagogical systems, in its family relationships, is constantly being totalized, and, in this totalization (through sin), people dominate other people. This, on the political level, is the oppressor state, the pedagogy of subjugation, i.e., a socio-political version of *machismo*.

If totalization is not thrust toward the future, is not detotalized, it goes on forever. Look at how the Hindus have defended the five castes for centuries. The castes came about through successive conquests in the subcontinent and were later sacralized. The Brahmins are the first caste and are on top of the heap, then come the military princes, then the artisans, until we come to the farmers. The lowest caste is made up of the pariahs, who have no respect for the order. This kind of system could go on forever because, once the order is sacralized, anyone who rebels against it is severely punished. The system is so well entrenched that any change from within is impossible.

The Chinese also, with their emperor and mandarins, endured for centuries because there was no one to detotalize their system. These systems prevailed for so long in India and China because within these cultures there was no prophetico-pedagogical and liberating institution like the church. What a pity that when we Christians are asked what the church has done, we don't know how to answer. This ignorance amounts to stupidity. Not to see that the church has been the moving force of history in our culture for two millennia! What further proof do we need than the stagnancy of India and China (before the revolution, which came about through contact with Christianity)? What this means is that these two cultures did not have within them a dysfunctional, destructuralizing capacity that would have detotalized them, thrust them into the future instead of clinging to the ontologies of totality found in Confucius and the Rig Veda. What happened? Exactly what I am saying—no one identifying with the poor, the outcasts came along to found an institution with a capacity for exteriority, to proclaim that their system was unjust and that a future, more just system is possible. (The only perfect system is beyond history.)

This is precisely what the Christians did in the Roman empire. Later they were able to do the same in the Holy Roman empire and in modern Europe. This dynamism was not due, as some seem to think, to access to the Mediterranean. In a sense, the Indian Ocean was better situated and China had a greater social cohesion. The Chinese were more culturally advanced than the Romans (witness their many inventions). Granted. But what happened? Simply that among the Romans there was a destructuralizing element, as a principle, a category. The other was respected; whoever went beyond the system was held to be of greatest value. This was not the case in India or China.

If the highest value is found within the system, who can move it? But if the opposite is true, a system cannot long remain immobile. It should be clear, then, that the function of the Christian in the world is precisely to destructuralize the totality totalized by sin. We can say that it is a rabble-rousing, subversive function, or whatever you want to call it. This is the subversive function of the church in world history and this is liberation. Go back and read the Scripture epigraph at the beginning of this book (Luke 23) and perhaps you will see what I am getting at.

But liberation from what exactly? From the prison of the system that is death. Jesus said, "Leave the dead to bury their dead" (Matt. 8:22). That is what sin is, the first kind of death. To die it is not necessary to be lowered into a tomb because the totalized system is already a tomb. And who will raise it up? The one who converts it and thrusts it toward the future.

This way of seeing things throws a whole new light on

them. There is a man who is of the flesh, says Paul, but there is a man who is according to the Spirit and who is reborn (1 Cor. 15). And Jesus says, "The wind [that is, the Spirit] blows wherever it pleases" (John 3:8), and he who receives it is reborn, raised up anew. We have to be born again! And this means precisely that we should get out from under totality, the system, sin, and walk in exteriority together with the poor. It would almost seem that we have been blind. It is the liberation of the oppressed from sin. Sin had totalized everything, "privatized" it. Sin had become minimized; a child steals a dollar from his mother to buy ice cream—that was sin. Going to bed with somebody you're not married to—that was sin. Everything was privatized, reduced in scale, minimized. We had taken away from sin its monstrous reality, its heartless subjugation. Sin is the whole political order as totalization, the whole ideological order as totalization, the whole ideological order that makes us believe that the culture of the system is the best, the culture that is touted on television and radio, in the schools at all levels, through books and every other way possible: That is sin. It is sin acceptable to all because all are guilty of it.

So, in saying "liberation of the oppressed from sin," I am saying what Jesus said when he quoted Isaiah, chapter 61: "The spirit of the Lord Yahweh has been given to me, for Yahweh has anointed me. He has sent me to bring good news to the poor, to bind up hearts that are broken; to proclaim liberty to captives, freedom to those in prison; to proclaim a year of favor [liberation], ... " that is, a year in which prisoners will come forth from their prisons.

Where the text says, "The spirit of the Lord Yahweh has been given to me," the meaning is that the Spirit enters in from exteriority. When the Spirit enters into the totality, the Incarnation is begun anew (it is the Spirit who begets Jesus in the flesh of Mary), a time, a year of liberation, an exodus from oppression, from sin, death, injustice (see Rom. 8). Do we not have here a logic that functions as a fresh historical rationality?

There still remains, then, much that we must learn to think about, that we must discover in Christianity. We must not allow five centuries of ideology to keep essential things from us. We have not been fed a pack of lies. But Christianity, in the measure that it continues to grow in history, continues to discover new possibilities; and we are in a time of grace. There is a "homogenous evolution of dogma" (to quote Father Arinteros). We can say that there is growth, in the sense of a continuous explication of the implicit. Indeed, I believe that, in these fantastic times in which Latin Americans are living, we shall very quickly recover a universal and political sense of sin and, therefore, also a universal and political sense of redemption. The search has been grand. In order to continue, we must accept the turmoil that comes with it.

The redemption of the oppressed from sin is liberation. (Redemption means saving the other by taking that person's place as a hostage.) Concretely, it is the liberation of the woman dominated by *machismo*, of the child from a subjugating pedagogy. By child I also mean disciple, citizen, patriot. In the phrase "subjugating pedagogy" I include all institutions that gloss over reality in a way that makes the oppressed believe that by nature they are destined to be slaves and that anyone who does not rebel against the "order" is a model of sanctity. This is a pedagogy that we have been made to feel in our bones and none of us can declare ourselves innocent (naturally I include myself). We simply do not have a critical conscience sufficiently clear to determine to what point we have identified a subjugating pedagogy with the nature of things.

We are talking about liberation from political injustice, that of the dominating class over the dominated classes, that of the systems that subjugate people. This is sin.

It should be clear that liberation, in the sense I am using the word, is quite traditional in the church, something we have always seen in the church. We agree with Gustavo Gutiérrez that all that the theology of liberation has done is to make us rethink all of theology by putting it in motion. Theology in recent times has been within an order that was thought to be eternal. But that is not so because the eternal is always act, process; the process is passage and the passage is Pasch. The theology of liberation is a paschal theology in the sense of being liberating. We leave sin behind and head for the kingdom; accompanying us as a historic sign is a concrete, historical plan for liberation. I take my stand on this, on what is profoundly traditional, going back to what has always been. But I do not say what many keep saying is traditional —which is to hide tradition.

On the other hand, it can be said that those who confuse their own present order with every possible order are indeed in error; they are traditionalists. Since they are so sure of their truth, they are critical of those in the paschal process as if the latter were the ones in error. They behave exactly like the Sanhedrin when Jesus declared himself to be the Son of God, the Christ (Matt. 26: 63–64); they tore their vestments because they thought they *possessed* God. How could anyone be God without their knowing about it? They were self-divinized!

Mystery as "Breaking Down the Barriers"

In the process of history the church fulfills the function of detotalization, which means "breaking down the barriers" (see Eph. 2). For Paul the mystery of Christ consists in breaking down the barriers so that there will be neither Gentile nor Jew but all will be "one." That "one" is eschatological. But breaking down barriers is historical. Indeed, breaking down barriers is precisely the passage; it is to grace someone, to set someone free, to set at liberty someone who is a prisoner. Hence the origin of the word "grace." Grace is like a free-conduct pass to someone in jail; it is the liberation of prisoners, or, as the army would say, a discharge. Grace, then, is the act itself in which prisoners are set free. They are told, "You who were slaves are now free." Now they have changed their ontological status. To set them free is to open the gates of the prison, of totalization, of sin, of death. Therefore to liberate is to rise anew, it is new life, new history, new person. All is new.

The Russian philosopher Nicolas Berdyaev says that the Greeks were unable to conceive the question of newness. They affirmed that things move, that is, it is permissible to have change *within* the system, but a *new* system, never! That would be absurd. How can there be any kind of newness in pantheism, for which everything already is. Newness in history is precisely the sign that God is the Creator and that there is a God who is exteriority. Because God is the Other, it is possible that there would still be something new—not everything is a "repeat of the same." If everything were a repeat of the same, this would mean that same is all there is. If this were so, it would mean that God is now the system and that is pantheism. It is idolatry and the bedrock of sin. The same is not all there is. The new is better than the same and it is future. Therefore Christians hurl themselves forward to what is to come (*adventus*); Christians never say, "All that is past was better." Rather, they say, in hope and faith, "Everything in the future will be better." The future of history is always new. The totalized world, then, the *flesh* of sin, is conquered by the ecclesial act of "service."

Liberation is the same as service in the original Judeo-Christian sense. Service is an act that goes beyond the system; it is gratuitous because it is done for the Other as other; it is the praxis of the servant of Yahweh. God anoints his servant with the Spirit and consecrates him prophet. The prophet commits himself in the process of liberation. In that process he must be determined to go all the way to death.

Jesus said that only those who lay down their lives for their friends truly love him. The prophets know that they will have to bear a heavy cross because to "break down barriers" of sin, of the system, is not at all easy. Many prophets, like Jesus, will die "outside the walls."

Jesus conquered death and sin. When he breached the wall of totality, the flesh, the system simply had to kill him. His death was the eschatological and salvific fact of history. There is a dialectic between sin as death and the death of the just as resurrection. In the same way there is an ecclesial act of service, of historic work, like that of the servant of Yahweh.

The church, in the first place and in essence, identifies with, and commits itself to, the poor. But if it is also committed to the subjugators, it becomes equivocal. If the subjugators take charge of the church and thereby displace the poor, the church becomes sterile. It is a sad day in church history when the sin of its members manages to stifle prophecy. Today we are living through a joyful time in Latin America because at this point in our history there are martyrs, the tortured, and the blood of the persecuted is being spilled by tyrannical governments. And for this reason the church among the poor, even though it be small, is sending forth its sign. Maybe very few do this. Nevertheless they are doing it, a weak flickering light but light nevertheless.

Again, the church will have to be with the poor and perform for them the "work of liberation." In fact, it has done this all through its history. In the Roman empire it put itself on the side of the poor and cast the process of history toward the future. Europe was born thanks to the liberating thrust in the church of the monks and farmers. At the time of the Renaissance, Europe, occupying the center of the world, proves through the conquest of the whole world that it is more *real* (fantastic but true) than any other culture. When Pizarro confronts Atahualpa, he is a much freer and more adult man than the Incan. He understands freedom whereas Atahualpa is still in the tragic world of the eternal return and therefore he is conquered. The Europeans are at the stage of nascent modernity, since they are no longer in the Roman empire but in the age of Latin Christendom, and therefore they are more real than Incan or Aztec—and, I would add, more real than the Chinese or Hindus. They are more real because they are more critical, more liberated. But instead of *serving* the Incans and the others as they should have, the Europeans used their strength to dominate them. There is sin; what God had given to the Europeans as a gift they used for themselves to subjugate the very weak. Instead of ministering to them as good Samaritans, the Europeans subjugate them.

At any rate, Europe was in fact more critical and more real because, thanks to the church, it had gone through many revolutions. The same thing is also happening today. Today again the church is thrusting humankind toward the future. And if Latin America is liberated, if the church in Latin America fulfills its mission at this time, it will go on sending forth its signs. If not, how great will be the scandal to the world! What a scandal for all the underdeveloped countries of the world! What a scandal if the Latin American church continues in solidarity with the present imperial totality, which is the center dominating the periphery! Hence it is clear that the Latin American church must give witness before the whole world, before China, India, southeast Asia, the Arab world. Its witness, its sign is: commitment to the liberation of Latin America and against the domination exercised by the imperialist countries. If the church does not commit itself to liberation, it will deny that Christ is truly present in that "passage," the "pasch of resurrection," in which the very essence of the church is at stake.

The Church, Liberating Force of History

Liberation is a historic passage and at the same time an eschatological sign. The church in history, again, is not a state. States are the cocoons of history, building and destroying for a while but being shed later along the way. Nor is the church the eschatological kingdom, which finds its fulfillment in ultimate totality. Rather, it is the liberating force of history, a force that will be spent when Christ comes again; his coming (the Parousia) is his only task. The church struggles so that people will mature and be able to shed the cocoons, the historic systems, and move on to more just systems until the kingdom, that is, Christ as Parousia, comes.

The liberation or salvation of history is the function of the church. This function is the detotalization of all finite systems that come along. These finite systems are never good in themselves but good only in reference to the future. The very moment a system sees itself as permanent, therein lies the sin of subjugation. A good system will look to the historic future. But a system is guilty of sin when it sees itself as the sole and irreplaceable system and therefore represses liberation. And it is here that the church must step in and "break down the barriers" and thrust everything toward the future.

In human history, in the Roman and Byzantine empires or in the Holy Roman empire, until we come to the "center" of our day (Russia, the United States, Europe), we see the church fulfilling its prophetico-historico-eschatological mission. More in one epoch, less in another. Today in Latin America it has returned to its ancient vocation in small groups committed to the poor but staying within the institution.* To discover those signs is to *know* in the light of faith the meaning of what is happening; it is to know where the eschatological remnant is. These are precisely the ones who place themselves at the critical level of history, who see a newness surfacing among the poor and the oppressed—the victims and not the perpetrators of sin. Those who place themselves among the poor are faithful to history and *make* history by liberating the people. Those who place themselves among the subjugators place themselves in what is dead, in sin, and they slow down, they retard history, kill the liberators, fulfill exactly the function of Jerusalem. "Jerusalem, Jerusalem, you that kill the prophets!" (Matt. 23:37). Read all that Jesus says about these things in the Gospel. It becomes quite obvious that he is inevitably destined to die.

---

*An eminent prelate of the church told me that the account of more recent events (1962–1973) in my *Historia de la Iglesia en América Latina* was a sort of caricature. I accept the judgment: caricature for a pagan history, because what is being sought are prophetic signs and not the mere recounting of events. It is "insane" history as far as professional historians are concerned (see 1 Cor. 1:17–2:5).

Being a member of the church, then, does not essentially mean that you have already entered into the kingdom of heaven, there to enjoy peace at last. To be a member of the church, which has a critico-liberating function, is to take on a responsibility, a commitment to the work of liberation. And right here we run into the most serious kind of confusion: To identify the church with the kingdom of heaven is to define it in terms of a ruling world order, for example, Christendom. In that case the church would be on the side of subjugation; it would become immobilized, silenced; it would retard history, kill it. Only when we realize that the kingdom is in the future and that to be a member of the church is not a signal honor but a responsibility will we see the church in a whole new light.

The Sacraments (as Consecration and Celebration) and Ministries (as a Function) of Liberation

Only now can we bring up the question of ministries and functions of the church. The church, as a prophetic institution, has distinct functional parts. But these "parts" in turn play a role of exteriority in regard to the very body of the church.

The modern experience of the church, European and even Latin American, has "privatized" the Christian person: To be a Christian is a matter for the individual. I made *my* examination of conscience; I had an individual or privatized conscience to examine. Furthermore, Christendom was identified with the church and, as I said, the reform of the church is at heart an intraecclesial and, at times, a political affair. Witness the "reform of Cisneros" in Spain under the Catholic kings. These two situations should be criticized: the privatization (life should be *communion*) and a Christendom that defines itself intraecclesially (we will find the solution in an understanding of the church from *outside* the church).

This can be presented on at least two levels: first, on the level of the Christian as one of the people—the *laos,* from which comes the word "laity"; second, on the level of the Christian as pastor or priest of the people. These two aspects go hand in hand.

The first of these is the ministry or function of being members of the church. We may ask: What is a Christian person, taken in the sense that the Christian is the anointed, the messiah? What does it mean to be messianic in our time? It means to be an alive member of the church in the function we have indicated. It is first of all to be before the world in a prophetic way; second, it is to be incarnated in that world; and, last, it is to detotalize the system, pointing the way to liberation as a sign of the eschatological.

What does it mean to be Christian? Indeed, in reality, one does not *be* a Christian but is always in the process of *becoming* a Christian. Those who are becoming Christians, as Kierkegaard would say, are not ones from the beginning. This "becoming Christian" is a movement of liberation in exactly the same way that we have been explaining all along. What I am getting to is a pedagogical introduction to the "use" of certain guidelines or fundamental categories of Christian thought.

Non-Christians live in a pre-Christian, pagan world. One day, the Word comes to them, borne by the church. That is why one person cannot carry the Word, because it will die with that person. It must be borne in history by a historic institution. Let us go back to the beginning of the description. One day the Word, prophetic and critical, invades the world and it points out to me the road of liberation from the prison of the world that has entrapped me. That Word is a call; it is a vocation that invades the flesh, the system, the totality. In a way I was dead because I was repeating the "same." Newness was passing me by.

When am I called? Whenever I listen to the other, to the poor. It is really more than a call, it is a shout, a loud clamoring; the truly Christian call to be part of the church is addressed to me by the poor but by means of the Word in prophetic function. It is the call of a poor person who loudly demands liberation. Again I say that the poor are the epiphany of the Word of God.

If we are not "convoked" in this way, our call can be a temptation and not a genuine call. Only the poor are the epiphany of God and whoever thinks to hear the word of God directly and not through the poor begins to interpret it badly. Hence there are many Christians who paradoxically lived a Christianity of Christendom where they made a "god" of the system that told them if they went to Mass they would get to heaven. That "god" was not the God of Christianity, because they had totalized "god" within their system; they could exploit people and still go to heaven. This is a contradiction, because to exploit others and still enter into the eschatological kingdom is impossible. If I exploit a person, I am divinizing my system and I cannot be in any other system than the one I live in. This is hell and that "god" is an idol. Let us never forget that hell has already begun for all those who are "following the way of this world, obeying the ruler who governs the spirit who is at work in those who resist the faith" (Eph. 2:2)—faith in the poor as the epiphany of God and his Christ.

Really to hear God is to hear him through someone who, from *outside* the system, tells me that the system is not the only possible one, that there can be another. Only when I become aware that the system is not divine can I hear divinity as exteriority. Only when I am able to comprehend the finiteness, the historicity, the inevitable coming to an end at any moment of the system in which I find myself—my home, my factory, my class, my club or whatever—can I hear the Word of God that calls me from the future. This Word is not abstract but is a summons to me on the part of the poor who cry out to me, in effect: "Do justice! because we have rights that are not yours. We have rights that arise in us and not in you. We do not ask that you give us what is yours but that you give us what is ours, starting with our worth as persons." If I recognize that word, I will be recognizing the Word of God.

But look how paradoxical this all becomes! Consider the case of the Christians who adored a "god" of their own making and who now suddenly discover the poor and want to work for their liberation. Now they say, "I no longer believe in God" and that they are having a crisis of faith. It is only the beginning of what I would call the political dark night of the soul, which St. John of the Cross never got around to describing. The trouble is that we don't know how to tell them quickly that they are in the preliminary stages of the encounter with the God of Israel, because the one they held to be "god" was no more than a fetish. That "god" went up in smoke, the same god they had preached to them in Catholic Action or they learned about in a twisted way from their catechism; but the one they were encountering in the history of the poor is the God of Israel. We must tell them that they are living through the political night of faith, not the kind of dark night in John of the Cross:

> On a dark night
> burning with anxious love,
> Oh, great good fortune!
> I left the quiet of my house
> without being noticed.

The house of the system was quiet and I, escaping through the door of liberation, might one day come to God. But to come to that God, I must pass through the night. And we say, "That man has lost the faith, poor fellow. He has become an atheist." But we do not understand that he had become an atheist in regard to the idol. It was precisely the preliminary stage needed to believe in the Christian God. It should be clear now how possible it is to see things in a different light.

When we discover and become aware that, in casting our lot with the poor, the oppressed, our commitment can lead to death, then we are on the road to Jerusalem, we are saints. And in order to be completely so, we must be confirmed in our option by ecclesial consecration. We are like the confused man Philip met on the road; after having explained the gospel to him for a few minutes, Philip baptized him. The man was already on the way; it only remained to point it out to him. The church frequently says that the politically committed person is running away from God. The Christian vocation, on the other hand, is always a vocation to the liberation of a people.

To become a Christian is to get to the point where we can hear the voice of God, but the historic voice. One becomes a Christian through a catechumenal process. The catechumenate is a commitment to an ecclesial community and a discovering day by day the *new* "meaning" of things; it is to know how to interpret the voice of the poor historically and concretely. It is not just a lot of theories we were once taught but, rather, a knowing how to hear the poor who summon us day by day. Thus it is that, little by little, in the Christian community, among the "people of God," through an existential practice and not through a theory, one learns the meaning of things. This new meaning does not become clear to me, for instance, because someone explains something theoretical and I repeat it back from memory (to repeat from memory is to repeat "the same"). This is the way we studied the catechism. To repeat "the same" is to repeat what is dead. The *new* cannot be repeated—we have to discover it; the new is the here and now, the how of responding to God. Learning by memory is a form of pedagogical domination. We cannot memorize heaven because it is in the future; we must be open and have faith and hope.

What this means, then, is that, in my day-to-day expectation of the kingdom and starting with the praxis of a community that teaches me its faith through its commitment, I learn the gospel. And when I have at last put myself on the road to liberation and am sufficiently mature for the process, then comes the supreme moment of my calling: "Are you ready to risk all for the liberation of the poor? Then you may approach, put on the white vestment, and be baptized. Baptism is a responsibility and not a prize." I am talking about the kind of prize a winning athlete receives after a race and, because of it, feels entitled to rest. It is not such a prize, and we should consider the disturbing parable of the Talents: because one man buried his talents, this was held against him. He would have been better off if he had received none.

Actually I do not receive baptism; rather, I am received into a prophetic body by baptismal consecration. We used to think that the individual being baptized was the substance and that baptism was an entitative accident. The grace of baptism was a received "quality." But it's just the opposite. Through baptism I am received "into" the church. I do not receive, I am received. Through baptism I am incorporated into the "prophetic body" of those who are determined to risk all in the church's liberating function in history. If I am not ready for this, it would be better if I, like the young St. Augustine, were to say, "I'll not be baptized yet." There is danger of sin here, because baptism is a responsibility, a consecration as a prophet of history. We used to think that if you did not receive baptism, you would not be saved. But there is a dogma of faith that says: "No one will fail to receive sufficient grace to be saved."

We have a contradiction here. Because of this, we have come up with concepts like "baptism of blood" and "baptism of desire." But because some neither shed their blood nor had any wish to become Christians, we had to fall back on something called the baptism of persons of good will. Nevertheless, I think we ought to look for a solution in another direction. The "Christic grace" comes to every person of good will and therefore each is saved as an individual. So, what is the church for? Precisely for what I have been explaining—to detotalize the historic systems and thrust them toward the Parousia. Were it not for the church, history would be irreversibly totalized and there would be no one to detotalize it, although persons of good will would go on being saved individually. The problem is not essentially a question of whether baptism saves individually. We can state this another way: Every person of good will arrives at the kingdom, and gets there through the mystical mediation of the ecclesial body, the church.

But, on the other hand, the church is an institution, as we have said, and in saying this, we are following the full Catholic tradition. Baptism is the consecration through which one enters the institution. One enters body and soul, with self-awareness and a sense of responsibility. Thus the *full* baptism we are talking about is a consecration that demands that I now, within my limitations, accept the responsibility of committing myself to the prophetic function in the world. I become "part" of the church. We accept the fact that there can be other kinds of baptism, but they must all bear a relationship to the baptism we are talking about. This baptism allows us to participate in the mission of the church. We are consecrated in order to fulfill a prophetico-salvific function to all humanity. Hence the pre-Christian, who was *before* or *alongside* the church, through baptism becomes a Christian by being now *in* the church. Baptism consecrates one; it makes one a participant in a body that is a prophetic institution. We will have to take another look at baptismal consecration on all levels—erotic, pedagogic, political.

Immediately there arises another question: What about the ordinary people? The people who were a part of Christendom, the people who celebrate a kind of folk Christianity. What happened to them? If we reject the faith of the people, we would be guilty of a *"conciencialismo"* (which says that only the self-aware are capable of entering the church). Where does that leave the people? We have something of a contradiction here. A "self-aware" faith would lead to an elitist Christianity. This is close to the position of those who hold that the Christian faith is always a "minority." But there are firm reasons for seeing the people as an oppressed people; their historic catechumenate has been a matter of centuries of suffering. This people was evangelized by Latin and colonial Christendom and therefore has faith. Theirs is not what we would call a well-informed faith but, rather, a historic faith. They believe in the poor because of their poverty. This is why they are open to the Word of God. They have faith but not all that explicitly. I would go further—they are on the way, they are in the catechumenate, they are in process. They are often closer to the Lord than those in the church who subjugate them. The latter have made an idol of the system, whereas those who do not believe in the system believe in the poor and are thus on the right road to God. The people's brand of faith is *catechumenal* and therefore rudimentarily Christian, indeed, at times explicitly Christian. They are frequently closer to the gospel than those who know theoretical theology but who, because they are the subjugators, have managed to make their theology serve the dominating system. Thus they deny the poor and also God; they raise an altar to the idol and formulate an ideology to which they give the name "theology."

Often the Christian people, poor and of the masses, have criteria that are much more profound than those of a well-informed but misdirected elite.

Between them and the *explicit* prophet, who is a part of the institutional church with complete responsibility and awareness, there is an analogy. The seed here falls on still better ground; it falls on the good ground in the consciousness of the baptized individual prophetically committed to the liberation of the poor. The seed will grow with difficulty in the consciousness of the subjugator; but even though it falls by the wayside, it could still grow between two rocks. There is still the possibility of salvation.

Harvey Cox in his book *Feast of Fools* reminds us of something that is deeply meaningful. Our opulent, pragmatic, consumer society has lost a feeling for fiesta, joy, play. In the Middle Ages there were certain days, like Mardi Gras carnivals in Brazil and elsewhere, on which all rules were set aside, and sarcasm and scoffing at everything were the order of the day. It was a discharge of pent-up aggressiveness, a time for breaking out, for pure play. Play as a thing apart from the practical, pragmatic, utilitarian order of the day (alienated work to make something to sell) is like a present, a gift, like an anticipation of the kingdom. From this has come a whole theology of play, a theme suggested by Nietzsche in the last century (and related with the Roman *otium,* the Greek *skhole,* and the Hindu nirvana). Certainly the feast of liberation has nothing to do with cold revolutionaries devoid of a sense of humor (who take life so seriously that they end up in embittered resentment), nor with the fun and games of the rich, nor even with the charming "feast of fools" of medieval Christendom. The feast of liberation is an explosive rejoicing, the contagious and enthusiastic happiness of a people being let out of prison. It's like a man getting out of jail and having a party among his loved ones to celebrate his freedom or like a soldier getting out of the army after a war and having a drink with friends to celebrate his return to civilian life. Or like in my country, Argentina, on May 25, 1973, when the people piled into the streets and shouted with joy because the oppressors were overthrown. The feast of liberation is the joy of an oppressed people and of those committed to their liberation. The sad people on that 25th of May were the oppressors.

The feast of liberation is not just a getting away from the routine of the daily grind but the end of the oppressive process and the beginning of a new world. It is not separate from day-to-day living, or parallel. It is a very real moment of day-to-day living. Rather than separateness it is a deepening of that day-to-day living. Of course we are not talking about the pragmatic kind of living the rich enjoy. On the contrary, we are talking of the burdensome living of the oppressed, which cannot be pragmatic because their *pragma* (their thing) has been ripped away from them. The feast of a people being liberated in a vibrant moment of their actual existence is something that can be reached out to and touched, not something abstract, put between parentheses, *otium.*

In the same way the festive celebration of the eucharistic liturgy should not be looked upon as play (the rich seem to do this), nor as a feast of fools (a surface phenomenon of a totalized society that wants to forget its sins, that is, its state of oppression, and that is why the people at this time can even poke fun at the bishops). Rather it should be looked upon from the standpoint of the liberated person at the very moment of being set free. It should be a true feast, having continuity with day-to-day suffering—the feast of Job, that of Jesus on the way to the cross, that of the Israelites in the hot, dry desert; a feast that is inscribed in the experience of the reality of a concrete, historical path. It is not a feast to help us forget about the oppressions of a system. It is a feast *in* the system but *of* the oppressed where there is rejoicing over past liberations as a promise of liberations to come and of the eschatological liberation. The eucharistic feast, visible presence of the risen Christ who reveals himself as eschatological, is the sacrament of anticipation of the kingdom to come, but kingdom understood as the end to all oppression and, therefore, sin. This is not the kind of feast where we get high on narcotics, drifting off into a nonexistent fantasy world. In this case the Mass would be no more than the opiate of the people. On the contrary, the contradictions and sufferings of living are realistically accepted by the sojourners in the desert in the festive spirit of a people celebrating its liberations.

On the 25th of May, when I saw vast numbers of people out in the street singing and shouting and waving flags (in an unaggressive way because nobody was threatening them, since their enemies were locked in the past) I couldn't help but say, This is what the parousia is going to be like. At the same moment, I understood that the Eucharist is the "feast of liberation" of an oppressed people being liberated in the infinite joy of him who gave himself to us as a Gift.

4

Alienation and Liberation of Woman in the Church: A Treatment of the Erotic in Theology

> *Let him kiss me with the kisses of his mouth.*
> Song of Songs 1:2
>
> *How can this come about, since I am a virgin?*
> Luke 1:34

My topic is very important for Latin America in general and the church in particular. My topic is woman's place in the church; my problem is how to phrase the question.

In the Latin American church there are 140,000 female religious. Think what it would mean if such a huge number of persons would dedicate themselves to the liberation of the people!

On the other hand, since theology has rarely been done by laity, the erotic question has been badly put for centuries. Indeed, there are questions that simply have never been brought up in the history of theology.

To pose this question of woman's place in the church, we must begin with the face-to-face, the original experience of Moses who came face-to-face with God. This experience can be described or analyzed on three levels because there are three possible kinds of relationship of person with person (we are reminded here analogically of the three persons of the Trinity). They are male-female, which becomes father-mother, parent-child, and brother-sister. The first is an erotic relationship, the second pedagogical, and the third political. And this applies even to the relationship of the totality of humankind before God, which is humankind's theological position, but always through the mediation of people, through "the poor, the orphan, or the widow," as the prophets say.

Let us now take up the first of these relationships, which even genetically is first.

Toward a History of the Erotic

How has the male-female relationship fared in history? For ten thousand years practically all the cultures that dominated the makeup of the Latin American world were patriarchal. The Indo-Europeans, as I have indicated, saw the God of heaven as a father God and not a mother God, and this tells us a great deal. Of course, as a French Protestant philosopher and theologian has told us, the category "father" is a symbol of the divine fecundity and creativity. Actually God is not a father or mother in the ontic sense because obviously God is neither male nor female. God is God, from the beginning, but was given the paternal symbol by a patriarchal culture that saw the father as having maximum authority. And because he had authority, he also had power, strength, the aptitude for violence. At the same time, all these cultures saw the father as the initiator of the procreative process. Thus God as Creator had to be viewed as the Father.

The Indo-European culture is ruled by male symbols that are in evidence on all levels. I propose now an example to think about: Consider Plato's book called the *Symposium* (or *Banquet*), a book well known in philosophical circles that treats of beauty, love, eros. I studied it in a seminar three years ago with a group from my university. We wanted to go on to things other than those immediately apparent. The conclusion was quite unexpected.

In the beginning of his dialogue, Plato tells us what eros, or love, is. There are five myths, or symbolic accounts, handed down by the sages of the past. He accepts that there is a heavenly Aphrodite and an earthly Aphrodite; that there is a goddess of supreme love and a goddess of common love. Love is the tension of "the same" for "the same." It's as when someone says, "There is my type" to a girl or a boy; my "type" is "the same" as I. In other words, we love "the same"; eros is love of the same for the same, and therefore Plato says that the heavenly Aphrodite is the goddess of homosexuals. Plato held that the highest form of sexuality was to be found among the Spartan soldiers. Remember that the Spartan aristocracy was made up of a small number of men addicted to war who dominated nations much larger than themselves. Young men until their thirtieth year were alone in the army; they were homosexuals.

So we have here a defense of homosexuality, love of the same for the same. But, he tells us, the man comes to the woman anyway and for that he proposes another myth, the myth of the androgyne. One of the sages who is recounting ancient beliefs says that in the beginning there was a being who was both man and woman. But the gods saw how strong this being was and divided it. Those who proceed from the androgyne are the males who love women; they adore the earthly Aphrodite, and this is vulgar. Plato believes, then, that the love of a man for a woman is secondary, and if the man must come to the woman, the reason is that "the same" would remain "the same." "The same" is the human race and remains the same through a new individual. Thus the man comes to the woman so that the man remains through the mediation of the woman. The man is interested in the male child. Thanks to the woman, he has a male child. The woman is of no consequence to him.

Plato, the wisdom of the Greeks! But Plato is not as clear as Aristotle. A pupil of mine is doing a study on the theme of property in Aristotle. And perhaps when he finishes his study, he will have to entitle it, *Aristotle, the Reactionary*. When you get deep into Aristotle, you are astounded at how oppressive of women was Greek wisdom. Aristotle, in both his work on economics and his work on politics, takes up the matter of the family. This is what he says at the outset: "Man is a political animal." Is he talking about every man? No indeed! For him the only political animal resides in the Greek *polis*. The barbarians are not men because they do not reside there. Neither are the slaves. Only he is a man who is a free male in the Greek city: Less than one out of every thousand of the people living at that time.

Woman, says Aristotle, does not have fullness of choice and therefore cannot buy or sell property or have slaves. Only the male can have them. Nor is the male child yet a man, because he is still on the way to becoming one through the educational process.

This kind of anthropology is strictly oligarchical, subjugative—a small percentage of humanity are men and the rest are not.

For Thomas also not all men are such *simpliciter*. In the *Summa Theologica* 1, question 57, he maintains that only he is a man who has no one over him (that is, a feudal lord) and therefore has "dominative right" over the servant. There is also a disciplinary right over the child and a kind of domestic right over the woman. This means that for Thomas also the male is the one who has full responsibility because he has achieved full liberty. He says that Adam committed the sin, and not Eve, because she did not have "full freedom of choice." In the *Summa* itself there was a certain medieval *machismo*. Sociologically it was bound to happen. Thomas was a man of his times, conditioned by the existing culture. It is interesting to note that this same doctrine was used to defend pedagogical domination. In the *Symposium* Plato says just that as the same remains the same thanks to procreation through the woman, so the teacher produces the same in the pupil. The pupil had contemplated divine things and then forgot them. It was the task of the teacher to remind him of these things. In the myth about the cave and in all the other Platonic myths we are told of everyday man who forgets the ideas he had about the gods and has to be reminded of them by the teacher. This is clearly a matter of pedagogical domination.

Socrates made his disciples believe that they were contemplating divine things that really were nothing more than constructs divinized by Greek culture. The soul, it was said, had seen divine ideas and then had sunk into the body. Socrates made them remember the things they had seen. But this process is a coverup. Socrates, with his subtle questions, gets them to answer in a way that someone of Greek culture would answer and makes them believe they are on the threshold of the divine. He divinizes Greek culture and prevents his disciples from taking a critical look at what is Greek. This constitutes the second part of the *Symposium*.

The domination of the woman—erotic domination—is followed by the pedagogical domination of the child.

The Erotic in Latin America

We come now to the modern age. The modern man who arrived in America was a "lord of conquest," the conquistador who lived in concubinage with the Indian woman. The Indian male did not live in concubinage with the Spanish woman. We have here not only political, cultural, and economic domination but erotic as well. Therefore, the American mother, the mother of the mestizo, is Indian. She is not Spain but Amerindia. The father is almighty Spain. Spain, therefore, is not the "motherland" but the father.

There comes to mind here a verse of Sor Juana Inés de la Cruz: "You men, you accuse women without any reason!" She, a woman well rooted in her epoch, rebels against the male who not only dominates the woman but makes her believe that she is well off being dominated. Sor Juana, on the other hand, as a virgin and a woman of culture, can rise up against the male because she is untouched by his domination. Here we can see the prophetic sense in being a consecrated religious who consecrates her liberation. This does not mean being married mystically to a "spouse" who spiritually oppresses her, as frequently happens. Jesus is celibate and not polygamous. He has no spouse. The nun's "wedding" ring will cease to have meaning when she comes to think about human liberation and not about darning stockings in a convent. This is the problem of 140,000 female religious in Latin

America who really are not what they should be because they are "mystically alienated" within the convent; nevertheless, they have been consecrated precisely to work for the pedagogical liberation of the child and the political liberation of the brother. Yet they remain alienated with a male who does not exist because Jesus is simply not an ontic spouse. Jesus is the teacher, the brother.

In Latin American history women enjoyed more esteem before the conquest than after it because our peoples—Aztecs, Chibchas, Incas, and almost all the Tupi-Guaraní—were *matrilineal* but not matriarchal. Among us today to be the son of an unknown father is an insult. Poor mother, poor child if the father will not declare himself. The father is all-important; if the father is unknown, the child is a nobody. How much further can alienation of the woman go?

In all the Indian cultures, however, it is the other way around—to be the child of an unknown mother is an insult. In fact, the insult of the pre-Hispanic epochs is "son of an unknown mother," because the mother determined one's place in the family tree. She was held in high esteem. A man once said to a Mayan king, "And you who boast so much, nobody knows who your mother is." The poor man was liquidated. In the *Popol Vuh* we read: "The mother and father of all have made all things." First the mother, then the father, as a couple. The gods are referred to in order as the mother gods and the father gods. Even in reference to persons they speak of grandmothers and then grandfathers. The same is found in all the great pre-Hispanic books. The females are named first because they are matrilineal. This means the woman enjoyed a higher religious esteem.

But then came the Semitic and Indo-European conquerors—Columbus, Cortés, Pizarro, Juan de Garay

—for whom the father was the origin of all things. They did away with esteem for woman in America and introduced *machismo* on the continent in a way that so far has been irreversible.

If we ask now what is the place of woman in our society, we can get an answer from someone like the Argentinian folk figure Martin Fierro, who says: "At that time I had my ranch, my children, and my woman." He puts his ranch first, his children second, and his wife in last place. He possesses the three as things and the last of the three is the woman.

There are even more interesting aspects to this question. Consider the tango, a song form indigenous to the people of our area and immensely popular. Millions of Latin Americans sing the tango verses. Medellín is the tango capital of the world. The tango is an erotic song with overtones of justice. One of the great tangos of 1918 is "Margot." It is a lament sung by a young lad from the slums. He is a nobody from the "periphery." He sings about his girl who was taken from him by an aristocrat who plied her with champagne. He is tormented by loneliness. The aristocrat makes a kept woman of the girl from the slums; ironically he demands that his aristocratic wife be a virgin because the women of aristocrats ought to be virgins. He then takes the girl to bed. The victim, of course, is the young man from the slums—a figure of oppression and despair. The tango is erotic social protest. The girl's name, Margarita, is changed to the French Margot—"now they call you Margot." She drinks champagne with the aristocracy while the young lad remains in the slums. He recalls the evenings with her and his mother, who worked by the light of a kerosene lamp, and he remembers when Margot was called Margarita. He is prepared to forgive the girl for her prostitution with the aristocrat. He will wait for her to return, even though she be old and gray. This is a clear instance of how the injustices suffered by the people find their way into popular songs.

The Being of Woman and Her Alienation

Ortega y Gasset says, "The being of woman is to be seen by the male." And women are to be seen half naked, in pinups and everywhere you look as "things" ... because, say the commercials, "the best *thing* in life is a car and a woman to go with it." The male is the subject in all this. The male is the one who gapes at pornographic pinups; the object, the one gaped at, is the female. Nowhere to be seen is the male. Ortega y Gasset has hit the nail on the head as far as woman's alienation is concerned. In the world of striptease, the male is in the "center" and the woman is a "thing" to be viewed. Right away, *ipso facto,* the woman is alienated by this because she is treated as an object, not as the other, not as exteriority. But what we see is not what is. Mystery lies beyond our vision; the other is beyond our vision. Ortega is simply being a masochistic philosopher in his flippancy toward women, indicating that he has not begun to understand the question. It is just as bad to say cute things about women as it is to say things against them.

Lamentable as is this situation where the male does not respect the female as his equal, worse still are the many myths that have emerged from this situation.

Consider first how woman has become a sex object. Man is seen as active in his sex role and woman as passive; her essential obligation is to satisfy the sexual desire of the male, above all in a traditional marriage. This makes her a sex object to such an extent that not only does she have to watch her figure at all times—it's not supposed to matter if the man keeps himself trim or not—but she is also assigned by myth the function of a "housekeeper." Thus the male is the doer in the "world," the one who works, and the woman keeps the house. The world invades her home through television, radio, the press, but that doesn't matter. Her third function, mythically assigned, is to be the exclusive educator of the children. Then what happens? For example, a twenty-four-year-old boy marries a twenty-four-year-old girl. Both having passed the bar exam, they set up a law office together. But when they are twenty-six the first child is born and the "normal" thing is for the wife to take care of the baby for a year or more. Meanwhile, he is doing well. Then come the second and third children. When the couple reach forty, he is a famous lawyer and she is a failure, and not just in law but in everything. Even though she has educated the children, the latter have no longer any need for her after their fifteenth birthday.

When it comes to the "virtues" required of the perfect wife, we see that a mystique has built up around what is essentially the oppression of women. There is supposed to be a mystique about keeping the house clean, about having everything in order for the husband's return from work, and about who knows how many other things that are expected of the obedient wife. It is no more than a mystification of the vices of oppression.

If, for example, you ask a twenty-one-year-old girl why she left medical school, her answer will be, "I left because I got married." If we asked a boy the same question and received the same answer, we would laugh. Why? Why do we allow the woman to fail and demand that the man do what he must do?

All this starts with the education a woman receives as a child. The male is encouraged to fight his way bravely upward, whereas the female is encouraged to play with dolls. Right from the beginning she is trained to be alienated for her future husband. Her whole acculturation brings her to this point. What then is woman? So culturally deformed has she become that the question is by now difficult to answer. Who are now the alienated ones in society? Women, 50 percent of humanity. And if the Bolivian miner is alienated, what about his wife? The man comes home with congested lungs, dying of hunger and cold. The only time he can be a "man" is when he beats his wife. How bad can things get for her—to be the oppressed wife of an oppressed man in an oppressed culture. Let us see how the church deals with this question.

Not too well. The oppression of women in the church is quite extensive, even among the religious, who for their part are dominated by their spiritual director or by their male superiors and on other levels. But the religious are essential to the liberation process; we must unleash all the strengths that our people and our church have if we are not to become mired in futility in sin.

Feminism and Women's Liberation

I believe that feminism, especially the North American brand, makes the following fundamental mistake: Feminists do not want woman to be dominated by man and to that end they call for "indistinctness." The Indo-Europeans said that "one" is good and "plurality" is evil. If plurality is evil, division is the origin of evil. Perfection, then, would be to de-divide or get back to the indeterminate original, to "nondetermination."

Feminism wants to do away with male and female and have only one sex. How is this to be done? For the answer we go back to Plato. The homosexual woman does not need a man because she can get her sexual pleasure in lesbian fashion. In the unisex world, all are the same, all comb their hair the same way. The women would want nothing but test-tube babies to avoid even pregnancy. With everyone thus equal we arrive at sexual nondifferentiation and we are headed for asexuality. They will accept nothing less than *totality*.

How strange all this is. Sin lies in the fission of sexes. Good, then, can only be sexual indistinctness. At heart such feminists propose to do away with sexuality; although it might not seem so, they want a kind of asexual angelicism. Once sexual otherness is done away with, each one finds sexual fulfillment within the self. Love thus becomes the tension of the same for the same.

This is all wrong, of course. Women's liberation will come not through indistinctiveness but rather precisely through distinctiveness. What has happened is that man has taken over woman, establishing that sex is properly masculine and that the woman has value only because she is castrated. It is the old problem of Freud. He says that a woman realizes that she is a woman when she discovers she has no penis and is therefore castrated by nature. Sexuality, seen from man's point of view, is exclusively phallic.

But there is a sexuality that is originally feminine. If man opens himself phallicly, so to speak, to the world, the woman opens herself clitorally and vaginally. Freud says explicitly that sexuality is by nature masculine. In his mental patients he had discovered that the *father* was in command of everything sexual and conditioned his sons for *machismo;* and the resultant illnesses of his clients —their hysteria, their neuroses—grew out of their *macho* repression. Freud had to say what he said because he was right—in *our* culture sexuality is masculine. But if he says *all* sexuality is masculine, he is wrong. Freud said what he did because he too was *macho* and he too alienated woman.

Women's liberation entails an opening of woman to the realm of distinctiveness. "Distinctive" is not the same as "different." What is different is *within* "the same" or within the man-woman totality, it is *machismo;* woman is the nonphallus, the castrated one. Distinctive is what is originally other. True woman's liberation consists in announcing that *machismo* is unrealistic because the phallus is not the only expression of sexuality. The male is thus dispossessed not on the politico-economic level but on the economico-domestic level, dispossessed of his phallic domination in order to be an equal before woman, who has her rightful clitoral-vaginal position.

It is now well known that the woman is more sexually sensitive in the clitoris than in the vagina. This makes her just as active sexually as the man and has a lot to say about the position for coitus.

These things that were never breathed aloud in theology are of the very essence of sexuality. The woman has every right to be as active as the man but she has been conditioned by the culture to be passive and to be the slave of the *macho's* sexual act.

Because man all along thought the woman to be sensitive in the vagina and not in the clitoris, much frigidity has resulted. Ninety percent of frigid women are frigid simply because they do not know about the clitoris. Faced with the frigidity of the woman, the man subjugates the woman as a sex object.

We will need to keep these scientific and ever so simple aspects in mind in our discussion of the erotic in Christian thinking.

The Erotic in Christian Thinking.
Liberation of the Consecrated Woman

"Let him kiss me with the kisses of his mouth," says the Song of Songs. If you read it, you will notice that there is no visual representation. The woman is only a voice that is heard. The voices of the lovers; perfume, warmth—all the senses except sight come into play. There is no description of the man or of the woman. The Song of Songs is a treatment of the erotic that is radically different from and opposed to Plato's *Symposium*. This then is our theme: Liberate woman not through asexual or homosexual differentiation but in sexual distinctiveness. Only then will she be woman. What follows is a description of three aspects of women's liberation.

Woman before a man is woman; before a father, she is mother. The first is an erotic relationship. Woman is mother before the child in a pedagogical relationship, a sister before a brother in a political relationship. These three relationships in turn are mutually affected. One relationship can condition another; the pedagogical relationship can condition the erotic, for example, and the erotic the political relationship.

This is to say that it is not just social or political conditioning that forces woman to live in alienation; it could also be that the mother, living this alienation, would train her daughter to be the slave of her sons, of the girl's future husband. The daughter is taught to accept a lesser salary than her brother in the factory in which he works or to accept that he will be a deputy and she not able to be, or president and she not able to be, or a bishop and she not able to be.

We feel confident that in the future we will see women priests, women bishops, and some day—and why not?—a woman pope. There is no theological or genetic objection: The woman is a human person.

Thus, since woman has a positive erotic role, she must liberate herself erotically from the male. Woman is distinct; she is as active as the male. Here there must be a strictly erotic liberation that will respect the mystery of each one.

Woman is also mother to her child on two levels—as a mother and as a teacher. But let us not forget that the father is father and also teacher to his children. The myth would have us believe that the mother is exclusively the teacher of her children; the truth is that the father should also be. What is lacking in child education in our culture is the male presence, leading the children to believe that everything about the home is feminine and their wanting to get away from family life. Husband and wife should give equal time to the education of the children, and this would enable her to devote time to her work and to her person.

Here is the place to bring up the problem of the consecrated woman in the church.

The consecrated woman in the church makes the gift of herself to God through nonmarriage; the relationship of man-woman is consecrated to God and therefore, mutually, the relationship of mother-child. It can be said that the unmarried religious is not a mother to anyone, just as she is not a spouse, in a real and physical sense, to Christ because, as I said, Jesus *really* is not polygamous.

Why, then, the consecration? To acquire the virtue of purity? This is not even biblical. Purity is a Greek word—for the Greeks the body was rotten. The menstrual flow was a symbol of sin and from this we get our phrase "the stain of sin." The same with male "pollution." But in the Bible all things are holy. Love of man and woman is a "knowing," and the person in the carnal act itself knows the Other in a face-to-face analogous to the "knowing" of God. So we're not talking about consecrating something negative—sin. There is no sin in normal sex.

What is consecrated is the erotic relationship and actual physical motherhood so that on a pedagogical and political level the demands of faith can be met with the greatest possible freedom. This is why St. Paul said, "I have no wife"—not because it is wrong to have a wife or because he did not want to be a father but because the constantly shifting demands of a highly dangerous prophetism would not allow this. He was a prisoner so many times, he was on the point of drowning at sea, he was beaten time and again; once he was lowered in a basket from the walls of Damascus. All this coming and going on behalf of the gospel prevented him from being an at-home husband and father of children. Their education would have been seriously impaired.

Therefore celibacy is not just for the sake of being pure but, rather, it is a consecration to a dangerous prophetic life.

You could see immediately the meaning of celibacy when, for example, in Argentina under the dictatorship of Onganía, a group of "Priests of the Third World" criticized the politics of the president of the Republic and went to the city of Rosario with the express purpose of getting themselves jailed as a form of liberation protest. In a situation of this kind celibacy makes sense.

This is what celibates are for, so that a family will not be put in jeopardy. Because they are free, they fear nothing and, consequently, are to be feared. A father of a family can't really go that far. There are times when he has to cool his approach because there are a wife and children to think of. Thus the whole idea of consecration is to give a much broader scope to the prophetic, pedagogical, and political function of the eschatologically minded Christian.

But what in fact happens? A girl, already profoundly alienated by her culture, enters the novitiate of a religious order where frequently she is further alienated in relation to a mystical male who does not exist as such. She is given a mound of inconsequential tasks that necessarily alienate her even more than the housewife. As I say, she ends up darning stockings, doing kitchen work, and sweeping the convent corridors. We never see her in any kind of prophetic posture, proclaiming the Word of God on television or in any of the media; she never gets elected to political office, never takes part in the labor movement.

Then why the consecration? The novitiate should be a time when this alienated girl is liberated first as a woman and then as a member of a society in which woman is still culturally alienated. Free at last, they can dedicate themselves to the liberation of humankind—woman, man, child, the elderly.

It is staggering to think what 140,000 free women consecrated to God and without family ties could do for the liberation of Latin America! By themselves they could liberate Latin America on all levels—political, cultural, economic, and religious.

All that remains for them to do is to go forth from their community to accomplish the work of pedagogical and political prophetism. Will enough go forth with a prophetic mission adequate to the demand of our time? Or will the majority remain trapped inside, to go on with their alienating domestic duties?

This is the problem of woman in general and, in particular, the problem of Latin American women. The woman religious is mystically alienated by a nonexistent male or by the spiritual director of the community. This spiritual direction should now be taking place in a community act called "revision of life."

In the long run, the woman religious must liberate herself from all masculine interference, even though it comes from the highest level. This is essential to the process of their liberation in Latin America. The poor, above all, need her liberation efforts. The liberated religious are the poor's best hope.

Clearly women's liberation is an important theme for any theology of liberation. Not that numbers are all that important, but 50 percent of the church's members are women and very little is said on this topic, mainly, I suppose, because very little theology is done by the laity. And they, having experienced the erotic, are the ones best qualified to tackle this subject. On the other hand—and this is paradoxical—no one speaks more lovingly of celibacy and virginity than the married Christian. But since the married Christian is seldom asked for an opinion, we are lacking a new approach in arguing for celibacy and virginity, an approach that would respond to the demands of Latin American liberation.

Miriam of Nazareth, Virgin of Guadalupe: A Free and Freeing Woman

Here are some closing thoughts on a woman of Israel who is also loved by the Latin American people. She was called Miriam in her town of Nazareth; Latin Americans, together with the Spaniards, call her Mary; the Indians call her the "dark Virgin."

Miriam, with a realism often lacking in so many false kinds of spirituality, clearly stated to God's angel: "But how can this come about [be a mother], since I am a virgin?" (Luke 1:34). One can be a teacher, but to be a mother can happen only through an erotic relationship with a man. In a realistic and exact sense there is no such thing as "spiritual motherhood" but only magisterium. Among all creatures, Miriam is the most perfect expression of creation. She was conceived without the tension of totalization, without autoerotic love, without the perversion that would lead her to deny the Other, Abel, the poor; and while still a child, she would do no less than open herself to the Word of God. That village girl, sister to her sisters, spouse to Joseph the simple carpenter, mother of Jesus, teacher of her son and, later on as an elderly lady, protector together with the apostles of the nascent church, is the prototype of anti-sin. Sin, we have said, is the totalization of the system, any system, any aspect of any system. Miriam is willing openness, and therefore radically poor, consecrated to prophecy, to the cause of the Word, her Son. Miriam's fecundity is correlative to her openness: "Be it done unto me according to your Word." It is for this reason that she comes forward as the "servant" (of Yahweh, a favorite theme of her son and disciple, Jesus) and yet able to admit that "the Almighty has done great things for me." Miriam is the finest expression of the soul of the Hebrew people.

Miriam, a free woman—because not alienated by a man nor by any kind of pressure from erotic, pedagogical, or political systems—risks all she has for liberation. "He has pulled down princes from their thrones and exalted the lowly. The hungry he has filled with good things, the rich sent empty away" (Luke 1:52–53). "To put down those who are above" is rendered in Latin with the verb *subvertere*—to subvert. In these verses of the Magnificat, Miriam reveals herself to be a teacher of subversion, of prophetic criticism, defining ahead of time the function of her Son, the church, and the Christian vocation until the Parousia. Miriam knew the theological categories of the people; her healthy, clear intelligence, unfettered and uncompromised, allowed her to speak the truth, to uncover deceit even though the powerful, "the princes of this world," were scandalized.

Miriam came to America venerated by the poor of Latin-Hispanic Christendom. The Indians understood immediately that she belonged to them, to the people. They honored her everywhere (as an assumptive substitution for feminine cults, a substitution that was correct and that preserved the historicity of their naturalistic myths), and they relied on her in their struggle to regain what was taken from them. They banded together in confraternities and Marian communities. The priest Hidalgo and, later, Morelos raised only one flag in Mexico—the flag of the "Guadalupana," the "dark Virgin." To the south Belgrano consecrated his army to Mary Immaculate and his flag bore her colors, blue and white, and those of the "Virgin of Buenos Aires," patron of sailors. Nevertheless that same Virgin of Liberation has been totalized by the systems. They have managed to identify her with sin, with oppression, making her into the "Mother of Resignation." Nothing can be further from the posture of Miriam of Nazareth, the mother of the man crucified for "stirring up the people."

Latin American liberation will be profoundly of the people when it is able to join the political proposals for liberation with the religious symbols that have formed the soul of the people. The secularization of the process of liberation is playing into the hands of the prince of this world, who is only too happy to abolish the religious tradition of a people. When the "Guadalupana," woman of the people and suffering with the people, again becomes the people's banner—as in the time of Hidalgo, who said, "The land belongs to those who work it"—then indeed liberation will arise from the very heart of the people.

5

The Situation of the Christian Thinker in Latin America: Epistemological Reflection on the Ontological Level

I will try to point out some aspects of the attitude that anyone ought to adopt who thinks as a Christian in Latin America. It is impossible to describe thoroughly that situation because it is like indescribable totality. The situation, because of its concreteness, is hard to talk about. Therefore, I will attempt to draw only along general lines the structure of the situation and the attitude called for, for purposes of dialogue and future discussions.

In view of the preceding chapters, I hope we can agree that we are going through something like the pangs of apocalyptic birth; and it's like this not only on the Latin American continent but throughout the world.

For the first time there exists one humanity. Until now there had existed closed-off empires. The Chinese thought they were a world unto themselves; so also did the Hindus and, for their part, the Europeans. Suddenly, in the sixteenth and seventeenth centuries, the European colonial epoch began and, with it, the discovery of other worlds. Thus humanity appears for the first time. Not humanity as a biological fact—we are all part of the one human species—but as a historical fact through which the individual has awareness and knowledge of other people. This in the beginning was disconcerting; the only thing we could think to do was to inflict on other people the vision we had of ourselves in our respective empires. Consider the Spaniards who came to America. They reported back to the king their doubts about the rationality of the Indians. They commented that the Indians seemed rational but had "thick skulls," which made communication with them impossible. Thus the Spaniards were unable to understand the depth of Indian culture. They thought they saw a man being "murdered" on the altar of the sun and failed to realize that theologically they were sacrificing him to the gods so that, because of the shedding of the victim's blood, the sun would go on shining. If Spaniards had understood this, they could have sunk the roots of evangelization much deeper. One thing certain is that today Latin Americans are feeling the consequences of humanity's appearance and, with it, the breakdown of colonial Christendom, and are being exposed to a new reality. It is at this point I begin this treatise.

What is the situation in which we find ourselves as Christians who want to look now to the future and put Christendom behind us?

The Meaning of Thinking

In the first place a thinker must know how to think. But thinking is a rarity in our times. Even under the best of circumstances what you frequently have is study. *Studium* is to go to work with a will on something. We can study, we can memorize, we can cope with a book, record it in our minds, synthesize it, explain it. Unfortunately this is what is done frequently in Argentina, even under ideal conditions. Our study is bookish and unrealistic because we are not accustomed to penetrating deeply into what we live and what we are surrounded by; but rather, from childhood on we study about the Nile and the Mississippi rivers without knowing a thing about the brook that runs nearby. How, then, can we get an idea of what a river is? In order to know the history of our people, we must first learn what it means to have a father, an aunt, a grandparent in time and to become acquainted with what goes on in our district and in the city, and then go on to universal history. Instead, we begin with the cave dweller. So, the child from the start sees history as a myth, geography as a fairy tale, and the nation as an ethereal, volatile, unreal entity. It is the general belief that study is the study only of what others have thought and written. All that the student has to do is accumulate content.

The Argentinian in general is not rooted in real thinking but, rather, leans to the study of the unreal, the abstract, the alienating. Thinking, then, is not a question of studying, calculating, planning. In any given school of philosophy you can count on your fingers those who think, and you will have fingers left over to count those who study; the great majority do neither.

We understand the things around us within a framework of existential comprehension, within the world's horizon. This is day-to-day comprehension. Everyone has this—the baker, the butcher, the teacher, the scientist. We understand things because we are human beings. But this is not the kind of comprehension we are talking about here. Thinking is not day-to-day comprehension, nor is it, as I have said, a form of study.

Thinking is the thinking that meditates, muses, turns things around in the mind. The sophist cannot think and does not know how to think. The memory expert or the person who has to read the latest best seller is not a thinker either. The one is a memory bank, the other a cherisher of the trivial. People in a big city feel that they have to keep up on the latest in everything. "While a dish is still being cooked," said Alfonso Reyes, "we take it away for a new dish." They end up with mental indigestion. We must learn to read slowly and to view what we are reading in terms of reality. If not, we simply keep ourselves informed with a daily ration of junk.

Crisis as a Condition for Thinking

To think is to turn over in our minds our "day-to-dayness," but above all it is to emerge from a crisis. But crisis is something we tend to put aside. Those who attempt to think about the where and how of their being without starting from a crisis point will not be able to think. Many perhaps have lived their whole lives without any crisis. Yet crisis is a sine qua non for thinking, and the more radical and abysmal the crisis, the greater the possibility for real thought. "Crisis" comes from the Greek verb *krinein*, meaning "to judge," but with the added note of "distancing oneself." Thus it is necessary to get away from ordinary day-to-day comprehension in order to see things "from outside."

In one of his early works Hegel refers to this fact. He also shows how the mind manifests itself progressively; it goes from consciousness to self-consciousness, and this leap is brought on by crisis. He describes that crisis in the person of Abraham. Abraham was in Ur, among the Chaldeans, and for no reason at all broke with his own and went off. He headed for the desert and was converted in a strange land. The words *Entfremdung, Entzweiung, Entäusserung* are already part of young Hegel's vocabulary. Abraham is a foreigner. It is paradoxical, but the one who approaches genuine thought approaches an inhospitable *(unheimlich)* place. In that sense we part company with Hegel because he thought that it was *zu Hause* that Abraham came to knowing, whereas we believe that people can know when they are not "at home," when they are in inhospitable surroundings.

If we believe that thinking calls for a comfortable situation where we are perfectly at home, we are mistaken. On the contrary, thinking will make strangers of us in our "day-to-dayness"; it will lay down conditions that will guarantee our "foreignness." Like Abraham we must remain beyond a mentality that gets lost in the thingness of things; we must see everything "from outside" —outside the obvious, the taken-for-granted, the traditional. The Greek philosophers called this *thaumazo,* that is, admire, to look *at* in an undistracted way. This comes about when everything surprises us. Chesterton, who was neither a theologian nor a philosopher but a thinker nonetheless, said, "The thing to be wondered at is not that some day the sun does not rise but that it rises every day." This is what is meant by being surprised. We are not amazed at prodigies all about us until something goes awry. One gets accustomed to one's surroundings, and that which would be the object of greatest admiration if one lived in the inhospitable country of thought is not admired. The attitude of thought is like being in the desert. Nietzsche wrote some of his letters with the return address "From the Desert." Obviously, he did not mean a geophysical desert.

Thus the situation of Christians in Argentina who wish to be thinkers is uncomfortable: first, because they are thinkers and, second because they are Christians. If thinking in itself is critical, it becomes ever more so from the standpoint of Christian faith. Faith, instead of giving us security, leaves us exposed to the elements. We should not ask security of Christianity but, rather, a scope of absolute comprehension that is constantly thrusting us forward. We said before that faith is a new "world." To think from the new world of faith is even more abysmal than thinking from the daily world. Thinking is to refer to the foundation of things, to what is hidden beneath the obvious corruption, to what is covered up by the dust of the day, namely, being. And when we think about being from the viewpoint of faith, the abyss becomes deeper. Its distance from us is even greater; we realize that thinking will never embrace all we set out to think about. There will never be an identification of theory with praxis. The dream at the end of Hegel's *Logic* is impossible because of its finitude.

This kind of thinking arises from crisis, the crisis that means our whole rhythm of life is changing. That is why Zubiri says that Socrates not only thought but made thought his life; to think became his *ethos*. Anyone, then, who thinks and makes thinking a way of life lives in crisis. It can be said that such a person lives in constant estrangement from day-to-dayness and can no longer eat, dress, sleep, or do anything as before. Thinking is the fruit of conversion, the culmination of existential conversion. One's life is changed. If not, one is not thinking. We have so often overlooked this in philosophy as well as theology. The leap we spoke of must become mature. And the leap, paradoxically, that comes about in the one who begins to think is allowed by the one who is already thinking, or should be allowed—but not in a theoretical way or on the strength of a theological, epistemological, or philosophical argument, because the beginner is still at the nonphilosophical stage. This is the question of the introduction to philosophy or theology. The beginner must be exhorted to conversion and death. *Death?* Yes, death to day-to-dayness, because to be ensconced and comfortable in day-to-dayness makes real thinking impossible; this death should roil our guts. Where there is no hurt there is no thought. If one does not live this to the hilt, thought will be sophistic, unrealistic.

The person in the street does not think. The average person calculates, weighs things deliberately but does not think, never goes to the root of things, to their ultimate dialectical horizon. For example, I always ask my philosophy students, "What is a watch?" After pondering the question, they eventually arrive at saying that a watch is an instrument for keeping time. From that point on I devote two or three classes demonstrating what is "beneath" the watch. If there is such a thing as a watch, it is because persons need to know what time it is. If they need to know the hour, it's because time is a value for them. Is it not said that time is money? So, what is of value then is not time, but money. And for whom is money of value? For the person who wants to "be-in-the-money," the bourgeois. It is not surprising, then, that the modern bourgeois would wear a watch close to his or her person like a bracelet. Whether I like it or not, my thinking arises from my ethos, from the ethos of the person of Moscow, Paris, or New York. As Pier Pasolini would say, "The bourgeoisie is found in modern society, whether it be capitalist or socialist." It can be said that the bourgeois ethos is so rooted in our culture, that, without a crisis, there can be no thinking. The Hindu monk has no use for a watch because he is not interested in saving time; it is not money to him. The same would be true of St. Francis of Assisi.

The reason we do not think on a daily basis is that everything is covered with the patina of the obvious. We have to overcome the bourgeois streak that is in all of us and put ourselves in a state of crisis. We must encamp outside the security of the fortress and know how to penetrate and dwell in an inhospitable land; from there we discover that a condition necessary for Christian thinking is to come out from behind the walls of Christendom. Its feeling of security is more deeply rooted in us than we imagine. The stamp of Christendom's security is on all our institutions; it is to be found in our theology and even in our Thomistic philosophy (not in the philosophy of Thomas—his thought did not enjoy the security of being Thomistic and he ran the usual risk of creative inhospitality by being an original thinker). This security is so deeply ingrained in us that it is possible that we will arrive at death before we can uproot it. Maybe those who are born after us will be free of it, but for us of this transitional generation it is too much a part of us. There are those for whom it is psychologically impossible to do without this security. If we take away from them their cultural scaffolding, it would be like taking away the skeletal structure of the body—there would be left a mass of blubber.

This is why many people in the church who are adults—we would not want to call them old—are incapable of a new point of view; supposedly the change would be too much for them. One of the cardinals at Vatican Council II said, "Our faith is coming to an end." What was coming to an end was the cultural support for his faith—Christendom. Any thinker who wants to be a Christian today in Argentina will have to abandon the false security of Christendom and be content again with poverty: a total poverty, the poverty of the remnant, of the "poor of Yahweh." The poor that Jesus talks about are not necessarily the economically poor but the "poor of Yahweh." They are individuals who radically understand their finiteness before the Absolute. They know that they are definitively open-ended, that they will never be a totalized totality. It is no trouble for them to bow low in adoration because they recognize their finiteness. This poverty must go very deep so that, like Moses in the desert, we can remain absolutely silent and then return with open ears and alert eyes in order to discover the real, the historic signs of the Lord's presence.

I don't know if anyone has ever had the experience of what this would be like. For example, suppose we left America and its European culture and journeyed to a country where we would have to speak a foreign tongue; suppose we left a Latin liturgy for a Byzantine liturgy, our own traditions for the traditions of others; suppose we left our customary work for a totally different work. Only then would we have the existential experience of being totally "without support." Because the language we spoke would be badly spoken, our work would be badly done, the social prestige we had enjoyed would be gone. We would then feel in our guts what it is like to be poor. Only later on would we become somewhat comfortable with the language, the traditions, the theology. We would get to the substance of what it was like before Christendom.

A concrete example: A theologian asks, "What is a parish?" The word "parish" in the Byzantine empire was the name given a municipality; it comes from the political and administrative terminology of Christendom. But what today in substance is a parish? The parish archives? A brick building? The parish is nothing more than the Eucharist in its communitarian celebration. All other elements in a parish can be changed around but as long as the Eucharist is celebrated by a living community, the parish goes on being a parish; anything else is added baggage. If we apply this kind of philosophical Christian thinking to something like the sacraments, we would at long last understand that the substance of things is very simple and that everything else is an unsubstantial encumbrance. We must strip ourselves of everything to arrive at absolute poverty. It is in absolute poverty that real thinking begins, especially if the individual has faith and, better still, if the person has philosophical skills that will carry into theology. Whoever goes deep down in the substance of things will be a true reformer, one capable of authentic *revolutio*.

Really, though, "revolution" is not a good word. *Revolvere* means "to turn back." But no revolutionary would accept that meaning. The better word we are looking for is *subvertere*—to put on top that which was hidden below. That which is hidden must be brought to light. Much more than being revolutionary, we must be subversive, like the prophets, not in the ordinary sense of the word but in its much more radical sense. We even have to subvert the revolutionaries because quite often what they have in mind for humankind is the same thing that they, without realizing it, are opposed to. There is a bourgeois soul inside many who claim to be revolutionaries and they cannot be counted on to resolve the present state of affairs.

Thinking has become in this epoch of crisis much more necessary. I had been trying to tell a group of Mexican students this very thing. But one student in philosophy said to me, "Professor, why do we need philosophy if we are to engage in a revolution?" After much discussion the student came to admit that, precisely because we are going to bring about reforms, we have to know what these reforms should be and why they should come about. The choice of revolution is clear to the revolutionary but this clarity itself must be put to the test of crisis if it is to be authentic.

Scholasticism and the Modern Period

One of the aspects of Catholic thinking is the unified structure of our philosophy and theology. This presents us with a problem. All thinking needs mediation. Thinking is reflecting. It demands a method, a way of getting to the heart of things. In the church almost until the present day the instrument for thought has been Aristotelian-Thomistic philosophy. It is a method of philosophizing that has become a system. Aristotle did not build a system, nor did Thomas, but others came along and systematized them.

In Latin America, and especially in Argentina, Scholasticism has been the church's philosophy. It has had two constitutive poles. In the first place, Scholasticism (Thomistic, Suaresian, Augustinian, Scotist) was the formative influence here; it was taught officially in the seminaries. But in the second place, along came neo-Thomism at the end of the nineteenth century and the beginning of the twentieth. The bishops studied it as seminarians and, in Rome or Spain, made a special study of canon law. The professors in Argentinian seminaries, until recently, taught only Scholasticism. The more outstanding thinkers among the laity, at the beginning of the century, studied only Thomism. It was a question, like it or not, of a Scholasticism that ignored, without realizing it, most of the fundamental theses of modern thought. With its essentialistic categories it "thingified" the world and people; being became mere existence opposed to essence; people were cognizant subjects in opposition to thingified objects. From that standpoint it is difficult to accept the "world," history, new existential conceptualizations. Scholasticism—not medieval Scholasticism, which for its time was quite revolutionary—must be abandoned. It has been no more than the scaffolding for the kind of thinking produced by Christendom.

Scholasticism as such came about as a creation, especially in the thirteenth century; it arose as risk and adventure. Think of the real, concrete, historic Thomas—the Thomas who was able to be a professor because his order had broken a professors' strike at the university in Paris. The Franciscans and Dominicans came to Paris and betrayed the striking professors. Their own men took over because the others were on strike. Nothing is ever black and white in human history.

Thomas taught and rethought Aristotle. He translated some of the texts. (This makes us wonder if there is not an Aristotle of our day.) He wrote commentaries on the texts, that is, until Bishop Tempier got wind of what he was doing and condemned his theses. Thomas was not born a "doctor" of the church but became a venturesome professor in proposing new theses to supplant old theses. For his time he evidenced a very coherent, mature, and contemporary teaching. Scholasticism, on the other hand, is only a repetition.

Today our task is to do what Abelard, Bonaventure, and Thomas did. We must confront our times, determine what methods are best adapted to understanding contemporary reality, and use them.

Modern Scholasticism is unaware of how deeply it is influenced by modern thought. Take, for example, a text as simple as the translation of Thomas's *Summa Theologica,* published by B.A.C. (It is not for me to say whether it is a good or bad translation.) At times we run across a sentence that says, "The *thing* [*res*] is understood" but it is translated, "The *object* is understood." The translator doesn't realize that he is employing modern categories about being that were foreign to Thomas; they would also be foreign to a post-modern person. Neo-

Thomism to a great extent is confined within modern realism. (I distinguish between modern and medieval realism.) Reading a book as important as Jacques Maritain's *Degrees of Knowledge*, we discover that there is continual talk of object and transobject, subject, etc. Without being aware of it, Scholastic thought reflects the thought of its time.

Beyond Scholasticism and Modernity: The Hermeneutic Question

The Christian thinker must go beyond Christendom to its foundation: Christianity. There must be a return to the de facto experience of Christians before Christendom came to be. We have to rethink the original experience of *being* Christian. What is the horizon of comprehension in which things take on a Christian meaning? We have to make a hermeneutic description of what a "Christian world" would be.

Concretely, in my treatise *El humanismo semita* I wanted to go deeply into this matter—a task that proved harder than it might appear. What is the horizon of comprehension of the Christian apart from Christendom and before it? That "comprehension of being" is different from that of the Greeks. It is different also from that of modern thinkers, although the latter begin with a "comprehension of being" proper to Christians rather than to the Hellenists. The "subject" on whom it devolves to transform substantiality into subjectivity had to undergo the experience of being as a person, something the Greeks lacked. Thus in order to get to a Descartes, it would have been out of the question to go directly from the Stoics and Aristotle—skipping over Ockham and Thomas and the anthropological and christological councils that spoke of Jesus Christ as a *person*. At the heart of every anthropological question is the "Adamic myth," as an expression of the "Adamic experience" of responsible freedom in the face of temptation. Heidegger forgets this, because the line he develops from the pre-Socratics up to and beyond modern thought skips over the Christian experience of being. For Heidegger Christianity seems never to have existed. Perhaps it should be the function of post-modern and post-Christian thought to reformulate the original experience of being in Judeo-Christian thought where Christian philosophy, if there is such, begins. Go back beyond modern Scholasticism to its foundation. The foundation of Scholasticism needs a new conceptualization. In this task we are in the stage of childhood.

In 1919, Heidegger, according to Richardson, conducted a seminar on the Hermeneutic of the De Facto, that is, on the interpretation of the de facto event. He had at hand one of Paul's letters to the Thessalonians and a few verses from Second Corinthians. It was a philosophical seminar organized by a thinker who had done four semesters of theology between 1909 and 1911. The problematic put forth by Heidegger was this: It was necessary to determine how the primitive Christian community —the Thessalonian letter was well chosen because of its emphasis on the Second Coming—faced up de facto to the future, the paradigmatic experience of life. In the letter the Lord is about to come and the Parousia is passionately awaited by those first Christians. That coming of the Lord as Parousia is what Heidegger in his *Being and Time* came to see as the parousia or manifestation of being. With the vantage point of knowing what the future would bring, he situates, from the merely human view, the de facto experience of life among the early Christians.

In 1920 Heidegger took up in another seminar the

question of Augustine and Neo-Platonism as a prototype of an inadequate conceptualization of de facto experience. De facto Christian experience was badly formulated from the beginning. Heidegger is in no way opposed to Christianity but, rather, to a Hellenized Christian theology because of its unsatisfactory way of formulating and conceptualizing. This theology and this philosophy are a constitutive part of Christendom. It can be said that Christendom managed to cover over the original fact of the de facto experience of Christian living and to conceptualize it in an unsatisfactory way. Although it may well have rejected certain unacceptable aspects of Hellenic thought, it neglects other Judeo-Christian facts because the conceptualization had no room for them. This is precisely the reason for our yearning to rethink and reconceptualize the de facto Christian experience today in Latin America. *Being and Time* expresses this critical attitude on another level. The question today rests with looking for new notions, concepts, and methods for explaining more in depth what is happening daily, existentially, de facto. We have just begun the task.

We have said that faith is a *habitus* (accident) of the *intellectus* (intellect). Furthermore it is said that it is a "belief," an "adherence to." At any rate the intellect, according to theoretical anthropology, has a very clear function. If, in contrast, we consider faith as a "supernatural mode of existential being," we will have to reformulate our definition of intellect as the ability to comprehend; it is no longer to be seen as the classic intellect but as something very different because it is an aspect of the being of the person as an existential "comprehender." Out of this reformation would come a whole new treatise. Be it said that such a treatise has not yet been undertaken but, when it is, it should respond to a number of questions. First, how does one acquire faith? Then, how should it be taught? De facto, life is the teacher of faith; we don't learn faith mainly from the catechism or a long list of other theoretical expressions. Faith is something learned in living. Family life as it was lived before Christianity, before coming to faith, should change after becoming Christian. How do I learn to live a Christian family life? I learn from another Christian.

Everything in the world thus changes its meaning. *Every* thing, because the horizon of comprehension has begun to change and thus the question becomes: How can we learn the new meaning that things have taken on? I will never understand the horizon of comprehension as an "object." If the horizon were objectifiable, we could apprehend it theoretically and by this alone become Christians. But the horizon is, rather, *pro*jectifiable. What we do every day is become aware of the meaning of a particular object and we project this upon the horizon. The new meaning of that object, in the light of faith, we project equally on the horizon and that projection is like an organic accumulation of all de facto experiences. The horizon is the fruit of projection and the basis on which I understand everything. Thus faith is learned de facto in historic living. A child learns faith, not in the catechism but within the family, in the world, in the Christian community. A Christian learns faith not in a theoretical catechumenate but in the praxis of a Christian community. The theoretical catechumenate becomes an explicit statement of what the person is already living; if the person is not living it, the theoretical catechumenate is of no avail. Out of all this could come a whole new treatise of faith as not simply a *habitus,* but as a "supernatural mode of existential being."

Thus everything would need to be reformulated. Original sin would have to be totally reformulated. Here we reformulate what Tresmontant, in a simple, ontological way, says about original sin: The person is in essence unfinished, and, therefore, by nature unsaved. That is, because of their ontological structure and because they are designed for the future, people can never reach totalized totality, to use a phrase of Sartre's. This means, first of all, to be in a state of peccability—the person can not-be—and, second, to be in a state of unsalvation —because what is saved cannot not-be. This thesis is metaphysical and not theological. It is what contemporary philosophers think about finitude. In the face of a clear and explicative formulation of original sin, Augustinian "biologism" and its own hidden Manichaeism are superseded, and, furthermore, baptism is given a much clearer statement: At the moment of creation, God had to plan human redemption as well; salvation, as totalized totality, is granted as a gratuitous gift in the grace of baptism.

But baptism de facto does not have as its only finality individual salvation because, as we have said, everyone is given this Christic grace in a mysterious manner. De facto, baptism is our entrance into the church. Baptism is not received; one is received by baptism into the church. Entrance into the church is not a matter only of individual salvation but principally the taking on of prophetic and historic responsibility to non-Christians. We have to reformulate baptism as being a matter of historic consecration.

After Christendom, we have to start anew to reformulate everything. I'm not saying we should forget about tradition. On the contrary. The one who destroys history for the sake of a needed conceptual reformulation is the real respecter of tradition. Whereas the traditionalist, in settling for the obvious, imposes what is false. If one repeats a century-old formula today, it has to be false: What it meant a century ago is not what it means today, because the "world" has changed, matured. Human truth cannot be eternal, unchangeable. Finite truth is intrinsically historical and, therefore, it opens itself progressively to the Absolute. We can say that when we situate ourselves in a way that enables us to comprehend being as it manifests itself, we are then able to perceive what is manifested. The problem lies in knowing how to situate ourselves. But that manifestation is always historical and, in turn, dialectically gradual. We can see, then, how many false problems are derived from an inadequate conceptualization of what is truth. The Christian thinker will have to put aside Christendom rudely and, in philosophy, the essentialistic Scholasticism. We now have to rethink everything "outside" Christendom and Scholasticism.

This demands a discovery of the new historic "situation." We are in a civilization that is profane, secularized, pluralistic, technical—but not technical in the modernistic sense. People are beginning to discover that there *are* limits to what they can achieve. People do not so much dominate things as they are dominated by them. We blast our way to the moon but in a very limited and careful way. We realize that we are not the masters of space but that space is our master and that we must humbly recognize our finitude. The moon has come closer but galactic and intergalactic space seems further away than ever. The moon was much nearer to the Greeks, circling around them in the celestial sphere. Furthermore there were only a few other spheres, no more. Now there are millions of galaxies millions of light years away. We are smaller than ever and the more our knowledge grows, the more insignificant we become. We discover that everything around us imposes limitations on us. Contemporary people are closer to God because they are closer to their own smallness.

The atheism of the modern god—the god that, according to Heidegger's understanding of Nietzsche, has died—is the death of a value. But the death of a value is not the death of God. In European culture God had become a value useful to people. What is God in Kant's system? Or in that of Descartes? God is a kind of idol that people have made in their own image and likeness to meet the demands of a system. If that god dies, blessed be God! Once the fetish has died, the God of Israel may appear on the horizon. It can be said that the "death of god" is the preparatory state for God's authentic manifestation. We have to discover not only a new historic manifestation of being but, along with it, a new hermeneutic. And that is the real and present task of thought in the 1970s. Ricoeur has demonstrated that the hermeneutic crisis is the biggest problem of our time. Psychoanalysis is a hermeneutic, an interpretation, not the kind found in natural science, physics, chemistry, but in history; it is an interpretation of the "logic of desires" manifested in dreams. History is a hermeneutic. Biblical exegesis is a hermeneutic of faith; so are the human sciences in general (psychology, sociology). So that is the problem—we have to rethink the whole matter of methodology. We must go beyond the phenomenology of Husserl.

Heidegger tells us that phenomenology remains as a historical given which the history of philosophy will study as one of its currents; considerably beyond phenomenology is the question of fundamental hermeneutics. That is the kind of hermeneutics we must discover. We have to focus it on our daily experiences in Latin America. Armed with an adequate hermeneutic method, we must get to a description of the meaning of daily experience, the comprehension of being and of things in Latin America. The task is enormous. Ernesto Mayz Vallenilla of Caracas, in his small book *El problema de América,* tells us that we must "let the meaning of the original being of America come to light through an existential analysis of our pre-ontological understanding of beings in a new world. This is the road we must follow all through time and history, the original history of America."

Here history is joined to ontology and the latter, in turn, is joined to theology. Anyone without these instruments is incapable of renewal. And this task of an existential analysis of the preontological understanding of being in America should be done generationally. What are the ultimate horizons of historico-transcendental comprehension which at the same time would be concrete and preconceptual? The answer to this question would be a description that would clarify for us what we are and how we as Latin Americans are radically different. We say "comprehension of being" or of the "historic world" because it is the comprehension of each epoch. Being reveals itself epochally. But in turn it is transcendental, in the sense that it is neither this nor that thing or genus; it is beyond everything, like a horizon. This transcendental horizon is not abstract but concrete because it is mine, ours, of our epoch. We must not confuse the abstract-universal of the concept with the concrete-transcendental of the horizon. The question is very simple; if I conceptualize a microphone in front of me, I interpret it when, for example, I say that a microphone is used for———. A horizon is intrinsically nonconceptualizable because if I want to have it "before my eyes" and I conceptualize it, I would be conceptualizing it from another horizon. It would then cease to be horizon. People conceptualize everything surrounding them as things "within" the world in a universal manner, but always from a nonconceptualized horizon. In the realm of the supernatural, faith explains this horizon.

It is impossible to describe thoroughly a nonconceptualized horizon; nevertheless, we can make an attempt. We can take a look at some of the elements of differentiation with other cultural spheres and arrive at some kind of understanding as to where the differences lie. But I repeat that it is impossible to describe a nonconceptualized horizon; the existential comprehension of being never is complete because being manifests itself here and now and, later on, historically, in another situation, . . . and still later on, in still another. Since the manifestation is historical, people will never understand being, absolute being, either in daily life or, even less, in their thinking. But the task, for its part, becomes more complicated when thought considers being as theme. It becomes much more difficult to describe that horizon of being's manifestation than to understand it in day-to-day living. This task, which is impossible to do adequately, can at least be attempted.

At any rate this task must be undertaken, however imperfectly, if we are to give an ontological foundation to every science of the spirit in Latin America. This is essential for theology, because theology also has the task of describing what it is to be a Christian in Latin America. A theology conceptually adequate for the de facto experience of Europe has only just begun; in fact, it has progressed much less than has been reported. There are great theologians who, with their "traditionalist" formation, are able to formulate the now, thanks to prescientific intuitions. Take Yves Congar, for example. He is stuck with a conceptualization from Christendom, yet he is able, with his considerable intuition, to formulate new realities, but his conceptualization is not really needed. If in Europe they are just getting started, how about we in Latin America who haven't even started? A conceptual reformulation of dogma applied to Latin American existential reality with a strong and disciplined hermeneutic method is today very difficult. An Argentinian theologian told me that very often formulations are drawn up by the "sense of smell"; we have to make that sense of smell "transcendental." We have to stop talking in terms of "It seems to me," and start talking epistemologically. It is a matter of method. We have to discipline our sense of smell methodologically. Otherwise our theology will be put together sporadically. That is the way it has been here in Latin America. Nevertheless, the recent "theology of liberation" has opened up new paths.

The Need for Creative, Historical, Concrete, Committed, Asystematic, Prophetic, Anguished Thought

We need *creative*, not imitative, thought. Many are carried away by easy solutions; many in Latin America, for example, call themselves Marxists. This is being imitative, not creative. They seem to be adopting a doctrine interpretative of a phase of European modernity. There is no awareness of the simple fact that the man named Marx was a philosopher and not some kind of god. He had his temporal, epochal limitations. What should be looked into are his historical *intentions,* taking on those that bear repeating. We should go beyond the conceptual formulation because we have gone beyond his epoch, the "ontology of the subject" which was the basis for his philosophy. All those imitative currents should be rethought from a much more creative position.

We need *historical* thought with Latin American roots, thought that begins with our concrete ontological horizon of comprehension. It should be thought that would know how to interpret Martín Fierro, for example, and have him say things that he has not yet said. For this we need someone with an ontological and even theological vision who could extract what lies behind and beneath *Martín Fierro*. This work, which itself is historical, traditional, and therefore monumental, would take on a truly universal aspect. Look what Heidegger did for the poet Hölderlein. Our culture would thus reach its proper horizons.

Our thought should be *concrete,* not abstract, able to bridge the gap between foundation and intraworldly praxis, cognizant of the restrictive situations in which we, as oppressed, find ourselves.

Our thought should be *committed,* and this is even more difficult. In general, thinkers are inhospitably isolated in thought but become quite comfortable there. In this isolation they disregard the demands of day-to-day living. In the *Critique de la raison dialectique* Sartre says that in the epoch of Marx it might well have been necessary to be revolutionary; but in our epoch the revolutionaries are so numerous that it would be well to cut down on them, and it was for this reason that people like Sartre dedicated themselves to thinking. Nevertheless, thinking can be the easy way out. The thinker ought to be committed in whatever way possible. We have no need for thought that is pure theory; theory must emerge from praxis. Thinkers who uproot themselves from the praxis that engages their thinking are also totally uprooted, without being aware of it, from their existence. They begin to be sophists, mere academicians; they adopt less risky but also less inciting attitudes; they fail to fulfill their historical function.

Theoretically such thinkers know that Socrates would go to the Athenian market place and risk asking the politicians if they were politicians. When they answered Yes, Socrates would ask: What is politics? And right there in public he would figuratively strip naked the politicians because they did not know the meaning of politics, even though claiming to practice it. No wonder they hated him and finally did away with him. Once he was out of the way, things returned to "normal." But his death showed that he was truly a philosopher. Jesus, a theologian, also risked his standing and in this he is an example to the theologian. The death of Socrates is the very paradigm of a philosopher's death; the death of Jesus is the paradigm of the death of the Christian, of humankind as such, and of the theologian in particular. These deaths must serve us as examples of what committed thought is, thought that grows out of crisis, that deeply respects the truth, the historic truth which, therefore, is committed to the process of liberation.

Our thought should be *asystematic* and open. It should never lean toward system. On the contrary, it should know that "knowing" can never adapt itself completely to ordinary, everyday comprehension and that its fall begins with systematization. To systematize is to build a scaffolding that impedes the growth of life. But leaving the question open is never easy.

It should be thought that is in and from oppression, in poverty and in injustice. These are the conditions of possibility for authentic thinking among us. Anyone living in opulence is unable to think; in contrast, those living in poverty and insecurity will have the ethos that will enable them to communicate with the rich as to what they should be thinking about: namely their Latin American brothers and sisters. It is very possible—and it is already happening—that the opulent society would turn to our underdeveloped world to ask for a breath of life for their own cold, academic thinking. It would not be utopian to imagine the time—and it is getting to this point—in which the people of tomorrow will look to our Third World, our underdeveloped world, because of its proximity to life and to poverty in which the spirit best shows forth its greatness.

Our thought should be *prophetic* in the sense that it lives in anticipation, running ahead of events (*vorlaufen*) as though called by the future (*Zu-kunft*). Christian thought in Latin America should be able to tell the *meaning* of the present and to say how, in that present, being arrives. This by no means signifies being traditionalists or aristocrats; but neither does it signify being like an alienated progressivist in a utopian "can-be" that never averts to the past. The progressivists who hurl themselves toward the future for the sake of the future have an interesting psychological and mythical makeup. They in no way identify with the sins of the past; they are innocent of them and, therefore, they speak of a radical, agonizing beginning; history starts with them. It is an adamic, pre-sin innocence. By contrast, those who absorb, take upon themselves, the sin of their people, also comprehend the meaning of that people. Then the "can-be" will be adequately grasped and will mean progress, revolution, but not utopia. The *ou-topos* is nowhere. Many of those who leap into action without historical rootedness are utopians.

Our thought must come from *anguish* because it is the thinking of an errant people, "errant" in the sense that it is wandering in error. Its destiny and being are hidden, it does not know what it is. Our thought should clarify this. The people look for someone to point the way, but all it has are sophists, false prophets, idols; it does not know where it is. On the face of the best propaganda, or indeed any kind of propaganda it follows this or that trend; it lacks a formed, critical awareness.

The Dangerous Situation of Thought

This plan for a drastic overhaul in our thinking surely will be criticized by the Scholasticism of Christendom. Conservative individuals lose their equilibrium when the earth as history starts to move and they feel they are falling. The manner of perceiving humankind in Christendom is static, like a monument on a pedestal. For the new vision of humankind hurled into history a better symbol is that of a jet. Speed itself prevents the plane from falling; when it loses speed it falls. History is somewhat like that—when the historical manifestations of being are lived and understood, history is in motion; its situation is "secure," but security comes from the very velocity of the thrust. When it is detained, its dynamic security disappears. When history causes the ground under us to move, the people of Christendom have a sense of falling and are critical of anyone who demands that they get a move on, and so they fault the latter as subversive, as destroyers of the foundation.

Latin American Marxism will also criticize this approach to thought, because it believes that it has settled once and for all the interpretation of revolution. But it fails to realize that every recipe imported to Latin America in fact is impractical. I believe that prophetic thought should cut a path between the right and the left, not in order to occupy a centrist, "moderate" position but as a cutting edge, the cutting edge of history. This is precisely what is meant by the call to prophecy. At this cutting edge, we will be situated among the left and the right and a traditionalism that holds that "everything in the past was better." It is a dangerous position to be in, open to attack from all sides. On one side we will be seen as reactionaries, on the other as Communists, Marxists, progressivists, or what have you. But one thing is certain:

Both the left and the right, capitalism or Marxism (not, however, to be identified with socialism) must be superseded, and to this every Christian thinker ought to be deeply committed.

This prophetic function should always be a matter of "universalization," a "liberating critique." People absolutize the relative. The Christian has a transhistorical vision, and therefore in history can always criticize the relative as being relative from the point of view of the absolute. It can be said that there is a demythification of every absolutized relative and that this is the valuable and ultimate function of Christian thinkers: They set out to demythologize the insidiously absolutized finite horizons and thus hurl history forward. For Christians human history can never come to a full stop. If that ever comes about, it will be because God has decided the time has come to call a halt to human history. Even though millions of years go by, human history will never reach irreversible totality because the history of the finite is unfinishable.

The Chinese empire closed in upon itself and for 2,500 years was able to live a kind of anticipated eternity; this was possible because "some thing" became absolutized and no one could any longer demythologize it from within. China lacked a prophet who, critical of the finite horizon, would have thrust it into the beyond. This should not be the case where there is a Christian capable of demythologizing the absolutized relative. But obviously this involves risk. Under the Roman empire, when the Christians said, "The sun is not a god nor is the moon a goddess," they were in effect atheists in respect to the empire's gods and for this they were dragged to the arena. They deserved to be because they were the subversives of the empire, so much so that in time they conquered it. But there first had to be a dialectic process of transcendence, and the Christian presence assured that Rome would not be like the Chinese empire; out of Rome came another empire and out of the latter, the present-day nation-states. If a culture has no transcendent emergence, it becomes stabilized because it becomes intrinsically integrated. The prophet always blows apart this kind of synthesis, thrusting the absolutized relative toward the future.

This, then, is the prophetic, universalizing, demythologizing, "liberatingly critical" role that we must always undertake. It is an uncomfortable position. It is the position of the apologists of the second century. Prophets belong squarely in their own culture, today the post-Christendom, post-modern culture, and they belong equally well to the church. The prophets need to belong to both worlds. This double belonging puts them "out in front"; that is always a dangerous position because one is criticized from both sides. People who are purely of the church, the clerics, are in an organization that allows them to absent themselves from the world. By contrast, those who are totally in the world, who have absolutized its values, live without contradictions but are incapable of transcending the world. The person "out in front" seems strange to these two. The cleric feels that the person "out in front" is leaving the church whereas the person of the world thinks that the same person is not sufficiently committed to the world. That is the position of the Christian—a person of *double belonging*—in the world and yet in the church. I think they will live and die as people divided, as misunderstood, and as forever losing. They will never see the final triumph of what they began. Those who witness the triumph will see it as something that just "happened," which will not be true.

If all that I have said were to be recast within the dialectic of domination (that is, the "practical" culmination of the modern metaphysics of subjectivity), we would understand the oppressive situation that weighs heavily upon Latin America and the need for liberation.

6

The Theology of Liberation: Epistemological Status

> *I believe in God the Father...*
> *Son... and Holy Spirit....*
>
> Apostles' Creed

I want to talk now about the "conditions of possibility" for a Latin American theology of liberation. The following will be epistemological reflections on this kind of theology. I wish to indicate that, in order to think theologically in Latin America, certain *conditions* must be fulfilled. Without them, no theology is possible here. This chapter will be a consideration of the method and the present status of the theology that responds to Latin American reality.

Imitative and European Theology

To encourage all of us and especially those who are not studious, we should know that Latin American theology is primitive. It is new, so new that in a few months one can study everything that has been written about it. To be up to date on European theology one has to study for years and years. But we are just beginning to take the first steps, real and not imitative and therefore not alienated or obfuscatory.

I decided to use the creed as a framework for this exposition. "I believe in God" is a matter of faith; there follows the matter of reflecting on that faith. In Latin America we are more and more inclined to think that theology has absolutized an aspect of the present world situation. It thus becomes, unconsciously and even unwillingly, an ideology, in the sense that it covers up rather than uncovers reality. If I take one aspect and affirm that this is all there is, I exclude everything that is not embraced by my reflection. I cover up what I have not uncovered. Perhaps all the theology we have studied has been a response to a certain "world" that is not the whole world of our time, that has not responded in its reflection to the marginal, the peripheral, the oppressed. Thus European theology—and United States theology is a reflection of it—the theology of the "center," has not discovered the sin of domination, rampant since the fifteenth century. Because of this failure, it has overlooked the kind of totalization that has taken place over the past five centuries.

Thus when their theologians talk about Christian *salvation* from within a system they believe to be the only one, they talk unrealistically. The system is calling for another kind of salvation. If I define sin badly, I will define the process of liberation badly. If I discover the real sin, then my thinking about liberation will be total and universal. So the question ought to be stated thus: European theology has held that "being Christian" is being a European Christian. Any other way of being Christian is beyond them. What is more, there is deception here, unconscious perhaps but dangerous because, until now, the theologians of the periphery, alienated more or less by the center, have repeated the theology of the center with two bad results: that of being imitative and that of pretending to have uncovered reality. To pretend to uncover reality when it is being covered up is a sin not only of alienation but of irresponsibility, the sin of "false prophets."

Modern Europeans: The "I" as Foundation

I will start with modern day in order not to go too far back. The starting point of modern Europeans is the fourteenth and fifteenth centuries. After having battled unsuccessfully against the Arab world, the modern Europeans find their way across the Atlantic and arrive in America. They are the Renaissance persons. They come to the agonizing discovery that they are not the only people. Russia and the United States have evidenced much greater power than the Europeans, but in the long run they are the Europeans' ultimate imitative heirs. We are thus at the end of an epoch. We must make a diagnosis of the Europeans' agony and find out if we are different from them and there is thus hope for us or if we will die with them.

Modern people became totalized in a way different from their predecessors. Medieval people, although totalized in their Christendom (excepting the great saints like Francis of Assisi and the great theologians like Thomas Aquinas), always recognized the other and that other was God. The critics of the Middle Ages prophesied from a divine transcendence. Thus Francis called himself "little brother" (which today would be like calling yourself "proletarian brother") because the lords of that epoch were the great ones and he, by contrast, became small. Everyone, nevertheless, recognized the other as God, and in the center of the world was the person, who was before God.

Modern European people, on the other hand, are centered upon themselves and, in a way, have made themselves god, denying divine transcendence. The Renaissance gives birth to the secularized subject, and that subject is divinized with Spinoza, the great Jewish philosopher of the Low Countries, or with Hegel, for whom humankind is nothing less than the deification of the *cogito*.

The European "I" is at the beginning of a process. In reality, the first experience of the "I" is an "I conquer," which went unnoticed by European ontological thought because these thinkers were mostly anti-Hispanic Central Europeans; they were not aware that before there could be a European "I" there first had to be, as a foundation for its potency, the "I conquer" of Cortes or of Pizarro. Thus the European "I" begins with the "I have sovereignty over all the lands" of the Hispanic king, ceded in capitulation to the "I conquer." America was the first conquest.

Later the power of conquest is phrased ontologically as "I think"; in other words "I" in turn begin to *reflect* on the fact of my conquest. With Descartes the "I think" becomes the foundation. He can even doubt his senses, the existence of his body. His "I" is reduced to his soul; it is found only in his soul. The "I" is the starting point for the unfolding of all else. If the "I think" is the foundation, where does that leave the other?

The Indian, for example, the African, the Asian is reduced to an idea, but even then not as something exterior but as an idea internal to the system "I" set up. People disappear as otherness and as history other than my own to become just an idea with the limits of the "I think." Finally, this "I" becomes an "I as will to power" in Nietzsche. It can be put this way: Things exist when I believe them to exist; the creator in this case is nothing more than an artist who brings forth the new from within. For Nietzsche this "I" is the complete man. There is in this a pantheistic vision of "the eternal return of the self." This "I," because it comes first, because it has been deified, and because it creates all the rest as something at its beck and call, is *unconditioned*. It should be noted that, since it comes first, there is nothing that comes before it, no previous condition. Furthermore, since it comes first, it is *indeterminate*, because all determination is within the "I." This is Fichte's position. This "I" is *undefined* inasmuch as it is infinite because all other realities are within that totalized world. This "I" is *absolute* and, therefore *divine*. This is what Hegel says about the primordial notion of "being-in-itself" and of "absolute as result." This "I" then is actually an "I think what is thought." There is no one else; "I am all there is." What there is, is only something that I think. Therefore, I am a "theoretical I" and things exist only inasmuch as I can think them to exist, as theory. I am "contemplating I" and things exist only inasmuch as I can contemplate them. Beyond contemplation, beyond vision or theory, is the not-being, nothing, that about which we can say nothing.

Awareness, Faith, and Abstract Theoretical Theology

"Awareness" is a way of being in the day-to-day world. Furthermore—and this is important—I can think about the awareness I have of things. Thus, I turn in upon myself in a reflex movement and make a judgment about my day-to-day conduct. This is self-awareness. I turn in upon myself so that my "conscience" will know what I am doing and be able to lead me, correct me, help me to plan, perfect me. This is precisely what Freud thought. For him sickness was a hiding away from awareness of the origin of the trauma. By identifying the originating trauma one would get well. It's this old business of "health through knowledge," a thesis defended by the Greeks. There is also in this a little of Ignatius, who to this extent was one with Freud and all modern thinkers in his insistence on the "examination of conscience." Salvation through *theory*—this is why we taught catechism as Christian "doctrine." The child *learned* the catechism theoretically and, presto! had faith and could repeat the "doctrine" by rote. It is a reduction of otherness to something known; knowing becomes important, as well as seeing, theorizing, contemplating. It is a reduction of exteriority to pure interiority of a world that is mine and, therefore, the negation of every other world as barbarian in need of being civilized. Thus Europeans contemplate their world and from that world see how they can conquer all other worlds.

Theology has used this same procedure surreptitiously because it also started with the "I think" but, in this case, "I think what is theological." And "the theological" consisted of doctrines, theoretical *articles* of faith that were thought of in terms of sentences with subject and predicate: "I believe in God." "I" is the subject, "believe" is the verb, and "God" its objective complement. It was a theoretical "article" of faith that I had to learn by rote. I learn, I comprehend in my world what this article of faith is saying; it is a "doctrine" that I know. All that is a serious watering down of faith, because when I say, "I believe in God," I am not affirming some thesis that I should memorize but something quite different, namely, that I, a person, recognizing that I am not all there is, open myself to God and listen to God's Word. But I am a concrete person and God is the Mystery; I cannot know God but only "believe in God." The creed cannot be known; rather, it is to be proclaimed, announced.

In the creed I express the impossibility of my knowing—that is why I say "I believe," not something but *"in Someone"* who is Mystery. The relationship is interpersonal; it is not a perception of a known object as in the case of an idea, but rather, of a person "before" a person, in a face-to-face. But theology had become a gnosis, a *Wissen*, a knowing. To do theology, one had to go into the "state of the question"of knowing. So to answer the question, What is the church? one had to consult the biblical dictionaries, all the formulations of the encyclopedias, then on to the treatises of the theologians and then arrive at establishing, laboriously and bookishly, the theological *status quaestionis*. All this was a painstaking theoretical study. The conclusions arrived at were the starting point for adding something new, complicating an aspect, and going on to a subtle exposition of the new discovery. The daily reality of an oppressed people, even the European people, was at another level, totally distinct from the *status quaestionis*.

The *status quaestionis* has nothing to do with day-to-day living. If *faith* is *giving thought* to a doctrine, theology, then, is *giving thought* to "what is thought." This kind of theoretical theology, which has itself as the point of departure when it propounds the *status quaestionis,* becomes divided. First there is the highest form of theology —dogmatic theology—which is called systematic *theory;* next, we have moral theology, which is the application of dogma to praxis; next is exegesis, which attempts to find biblical backing for the first principles of theoretical argumentation; further on comes pastoral theology, which is a study of how to convert people and bring them into the kingdom; then homiletics, which is the study of how to use rhetorical techniques to stir people; then there is historical theology, which anecdotally describes the history of the church.

Theology is thus broken up into pieces that are all

founded on theoretical principles whose *status quaestionis* is derived from theology itself.

The result of this process has been that the other, the poor, those who are the epiphany of God, have been reduced to a *cogitatum* ("that which is thought"). About the other, much can now be said and thought. But if "I think" about someone and know him, I cannot ask him, Who are you? I don't ask, Who are you? if I know who someone is, nor do I ask, How are you? when I know how the person is. If I make that person an object, *cogitatum*, if I know the other, I cannot believe in that other or have the experience of face-to-face. Only if the other is *beyond* my understanding and knowing can I humbly bow before that other as before something sacred and ask, Who are you? And how are you? Summon me out of my finitude to serve and, therefore, to grow!

The other was destroyed by Europe because, as I have already pointed out, the other was interiorized in a world system. Trent, echoing Paul, said that faith comes from hearing (*ex auditum*) but, in fact, the men of Trent listened only to the Europeans. Did they know nothing about the Indians, about the blacks sold as slaves, about the Asians? Just like succeeding councils, Trent was interested only in intra-European and intra-Latin questions; the Byzantine problem was not even on the agenda and at the height of the sixteenth century the Lutherans were being dismissed. We see then just how far they went in negating the other and how, imperceptibly, the church took on the totalization of the center and the subjugation of the poor. Bartolomé de las Casas cried out: "They are killing the Indians and reducing them to the most frightening kind of subjugation and slavery." But Europe didn't really believe this; it was not interested (apart from seeing the situation as an excuse for criticizing Spain). The intellectuals would have said that

Bartolomé was paranoid. He was a voice crying in the desert, but there were no ears to hear him. *Ex auditum* was solemnly stated but in fact was ignored.

Thus the sin of subjugation went undiscovered and therefore the comprehensive sin of this whole historical epoch went undiscovered. Since the concrete meaning of salvation and redemption also went undiscovered, the horizon of Christian living becomes privatized, or, at best, was lived out within the national horizon. Thus the Spaniards under the Catholic kings saw the internal sins of the Iberian peninsula; the French under the most Christian of kings saw their side of it; the Germans and their princes likewise. Redemption is considered within the boundaries of the nation, or within Europe, but, at any rate, within privatized boundaries. The European theologians themselves have been trying to review this situation, and out of their efforts should come important new theological considerations.

Solipsism in Existential Theology

First Rahner, then Schillebeeckx and the whole trend of what can be called existential theology begin with the following suppositions. They have studied Heidegger and, like Heidegger, have risen up against modern thought. For them "to think" does not come first but, rather, the "to be-in-a-world," to be *in* that in which some day I will begin "to think" about. To think is not the foundation; "to be-in-a-world" is. I am first of all and every day in Buenos Aires, in Argentina, in Latin America; some day, due to some crisis situation, I will start thinking. But the problem of thinking is secondary to *understanding* the day-to-day world. This theology, that of Rahner and Schillebeeckx, proposes the following: First, being is in the existential world; then comes reflection about the existential, or day-to-day existence, and this is thinking. This kind of thinking is called not existential but "existentiary." Consult any of their books and you will read that faith is an existential position and theology an existentiary position because theology is a reflection on day-to-dayness. This is very important because traditional modern theology, including neo-Scholasticism, frequently started with one's own experience of consciousness as thinking in order to think theologically about something; their starting point was theology. Whereas Rahner and the others now recognize that the starting point has to be day-to-dayness in order to come up with a way of thinking about day-to-dayness. There is great interest in this review of existential theology.

Where should the advancement of Latin American theology be based? In the idea that "to be-in-the-world" is the same for all Christians. The "world," and therefore "to be-in-the-world," is the same experience for all Christians.

In my book *History and the Theology of Liberation* (Maryknoll, New York: Orbis Books, 1976), I explained the significance of "to be-in-the-world" that was pre-Christian, and how faith is a *new* light in which the world is seen as a new world. It is a new existence because I see everything differently, I discover a new meaning to things.

It is affirmed that the world is *one*. But this is a mistake because what is really being affirmed is that that one world is the European world. Since the Latin American world is *beyond* the European world, as something "barbarian," it is not recognized in its exteriority. So we again have the indeterminate "I think." Now the "to think" is determined by a world, but the European world is the indeterminate, the foundation. Latin American theology says No! That world is also conditioned and conditions others; it is not the only world. "To-be-Christian" in the center is not the same as "to-be-Christian" on the periphery. It is not the same to think from the center as to think out of oppression or to think about the periphery from the periphery itself.

The worst comes, though, when the periphery thinks European thought and discovers European reality in the belief that it has found its own reality. This is the supreme theological alienation that afflicts so many in Latin America. There is a double fallacy here: in the first place, that of believing its thinking to be the only thinking; second, in believing that the European reality is identical with ours and that therefore our reality doesn't really exist. So, of course, there would not, and could not be, a Latin American theology; there would only be one theology—the European, which, furthermore, is universal because the "to be-Christian" can only mean "to be-European." At the present time in Latin America, the greatest danger of rootlessness is to be found in repeating uncritically the progressivist theology of Europe.

Lack of Historico-Political Mediation in the "Theology of Hope"

Let us go one step further and consider the thought of Moltmann in his *Theology of Hope*. Starting with the thinking of Ernst Bloch about hope, he demonstrates that the world is totalized as a world of "remembrance of the same." For him the essence of Christianity is hope, hope for the kingdom. No system can come forward as the ultimate except the kingdom. Thus there are two kingdoms—the prevailing present kingdom and the eschatological kingdom. He shows that those who allow themselves to be locked off in the latter kingdom commit an idolatrous act; and only by hoping for the future kingdom can we challenge the system and open ourselves to the Parousia, to the utopian. What kind of critique can be brought against this theology? Very simply, he conjures away a third terminus by using only two poles, thus reaffirming the status quo. (By 1974 Moltmann had begun to modify this thesis, however.) See how a logic of hope that is not sufficiently historical functions. Simply by saying that we must hope for the kingdom allows me to open myself to God. But if I speak of hope as eschatological hope, how, in fact, can I signify this through my commitments? The only way would be to work away in hope. But in the presence of the historical visible kingdom, how do I give witness to the eschatological? In the presence of the economic, the political, the cultural, how do I symbolize or manifest the eschatological kingdom? Moltmann ends in saying very little, a kind of justification of professional ethics through which all do their duty in hope without the need to question radically the totality of the system. Between the prevailing system and the kingdom, however, there is a third aspect that I have been talking about all along; this is the historical plan for liberation which is neither the prevailing kingdom of the moment nor the eschatological kingdom.

It is not sufficient only to speak of hope beyond the status quo. Even though we say we are hoping for the kingdom, we are reaffirming and sacralizing the status quo by not risking all historically in a project for the future, by not becoming empirically through our praxis a dysfunctional factor within the system. We go to Mass for the eucharistic celebration and hope even more fervently for the kingdom; we pray and come away from the community enthused. We work all week, perhaps harder than the rest, but we do not question the system as such.

Epistemological Status   161

Whoever affirms the system in a private way (even though it be social) with the hope of the kingdom but in fact calls for no historical, empirical upsetting of the system, with the purpose of thrusting it anew toward a historical project for liberation, reaffirms the system. The theologians are in the center, without realizing it, living in the best of all possible worlds. Afterward comes the kingdom; there is no *new* plan for liberation on the horizon. About all the theologians can do for their contemporaries is free them from the bonds of the consumer society. Thus Moltmann as well as Marcuse and the others who want to challenge people from within the superconsumer society come up with the monks' remedy of retiring from the world, and thus we have the emergence of the hippie. The hippie is one who essentially says No to the system and retires from it. It is the *play* of Cox's theology, which comes from Nietzsche. But to retire from the system is an epiphenomenon of the system and does not as such overcome it; it does not call it into question. Hippies may lead a more human life, but they do not affect the totality of sin as such. Their lifestyle represents an extrinsic and perhaps symbolic motivation for survival.

In contrast, the concrete process of liberation of the underdeveloped nations challenges the totality of the system, not just as external criticism but also as an internal tearing apart of the totality. Hence the fact of self-redefinition with respect to the system in the light of faith and hope in God is not the same as believing and hoping in God while totally dedicating oneself to a concrete system of historical liberation. Moltmann, then, although he poses the question of working out a plan for the future, does not take up the phenomenon of the historical project for *liberation* that calls for a complete economic, political, and cultural commitment. Because he fails in this, he has disemboweled hope and even turned it into opium.

Lack of International Vision in Political Theology

In the same way we could find fault with the critique that Johann Metz puts forward in his political theology. Metz says, and rightly so, that traditional theology has been privatized thinking, proper to the individual who fulfilled a function in the church and in society without any critical sense. Theology, then, was an accomplice of the society. Beginning with such reflections as those of Henri De Lubac in *Catholicism,* we can show that there is not a single Christian dogma that is private; all are social. In Christianity the individual is not considered an autonomous totality but as exteriority or as part of a community. But Metz goes further than De Lubac. He demonstrates that dogma is not only social but that the function of Christian faith and theology is a critico-liberating function for the world it inhabits. This is the theology we are concerned with; it is a reflection on day-to-dayness that is critical and deprivatizing and points out the communitarian demands upon people at all levels.

The drawback is that the critique is done from the horizon of a nation and, to be even more concrete, of a *European* nation. He talks about a *whole* in which theology should fulfill its critical function. But what is that whole? That of one nation. Could we not ask him: Why do you not propound this critique on an international level, where there are peoples on the periphery and nations in the center? In this way his prophetic critique could become a critique on the domination of the center countries, of imperialism, of exploitation of poor peoples.

Where is there a critique of imperialism in the sense of worldwide exploitation of person by person? But here Metz provides no critique because he is very much a part of the German national reality and never achieves a problematization of the international horizon within which we live, but only of "his" national world. He finds support in the world of the center for his critique. But it is not the same if you are on the periphery.

Finding ourselves on the periphery, the whole that we look at is not the center but really the totality of the present world system. Being poor, we are closer to *reality* than those who are in the center, in the money. Suddenly, poverty becomes a great blessing even for theology as well as for Christian living, because we can glimpse the next system aborning and we can know how to commit ourselves to its coming. Those who have not become aware of domination are unable to call into question the international whole, which is the whole of the world. European political theology has called into question only the national *whole*. But in doing so, it approves that which makes that national whole what it is; this is to say that it approves the domination wreaked on other peoples and fudges its criticism. Its criticism, being national, is not sufficiently liberating; it becomes ideological again, because it criticizes "part" of the system and not the totality of the German national system, for example, as a country of the center.

Peoples' Struggle Before Class Struggle

The French theologian of Italian origin, Giulio Girardi, speaks of a theology of European liberation and "class struggle." I believe his position to be highly important because he shows how theology can fulfill a critico-social and even revolutionary function, since the struggle among people, subjugated and subjugating, is a concrete reality. But he doesn't explain clearly the origin of the struggle. The *origin* of the class struggle is a first fact of history, but the struggle itself is a second fact. First, people are in the totality; they dominate others, alienate them. When the dominated become aware of their condition of servitude, there is born in them the "will to freedom" and they set out along the road to liberation. Once they do, repression occurs. The response to repression is war, struggle. Class struggle appears only after the "will to freedom" and the "love of justice." First you have the love of justice for the poor, a commitment to them. Once in motion, it starts the struggle. Struggle is the outcome of sin, a frequent theme of the Bible. The class struggle is a fact but only a secondary fact. This is the difference between a Marxist and a Christian interpretation.

Struggle is the outcome of sin, but the two opponents are not equally in the right, nor are both sides bad. Those who attack as subjugators are perverse; they are "angels" of the "prince of this world." The subjugated who defend themselves are good; they are liberation heroes. The liberation theologians of the center are concerned about the poor of the center, who are the laboring class of Germany, France, the United States, but they do not advert to the fact that there is an essential difference between the poor of the center and the poor of the "world," those on the periphery. The North American miner is poor but he makes five dollars an hour; a Bolivian worker earns a dollar a day—forty times less! The difference is much too great. North American workers are part of the system of domination that they benefit by, and that is why at heart they are opposed to the liberation of the Bolivian worker. If Bolivia were to be liberated, North American prosperity could be in trouble and so would the worker. Therefore, the worker in the center is

willing to go along with the exploitation of the worker on the periphery.
These facts are overlooked by the liberation theologians of the center. Latin American liberation is more radical and has different motivations. It should be clear that the case is different.

Liberation Theology?

It is time now to go into the origin of "liberation theology." Gustavo Gutiérrez was mainly responsible for its origin when, a few years ago, he began to ask himself, "Is there a theology of development" or "a theology of liberation"? From the model of development, there arose a theology of developmentalism, which had as its model the center. Liberation theology arises from the discovery of the fact of dependence. Now the model is no longer imitation of the center but, rather, the proposal of a new person based on an understanding of the structure of the world system. It is a theology that is much more radical, universal, and world-embracing, not just one new aspect but a total transformation of theological reflection.

Gutiérrez was the first to begin the soundings for this new theology, and his starting point was the one great fact of poverty. The Medellín pronouncements on poverty, which were the work mainly of Gutiérrez, are important because of their revelation of the poor as oppressed. The poor revealed as exteriority is the beginning of the reflective process that concerns us here.

Thus we have a whole new approach to theology, epistemologically because of the formulation of the question of dependence, spiritually because of the discovery of the countenance of today's poor. It is along this path that Hugo Assmann, for example, with his fine grasp of European theology, begins his critique of European theologians, showing step by step that that theology has confined itself to a given horizon to the point of becoming ideology. European theology is not for the periphery, not for or from the barbarians. What we need is some kind of "suspicionometer"; we need to be suspicious of what is hidden in many of their reflections. Our theology will be much more critical than theirs, not because we are more intelligent, nor because we would have more theological tools, but simply because we are victims of the system and because we are on the outside.

A beggar, for example, sees the color on the outside of the rich man's house *from* the outside, something the rich man on the inside doesn't see. We have a better view of the house of the center because we live on the outside. We are not stronger but weaker. But in this case weakness is an asset. Our theology engages in criticism of the theology of the center precisely because ours is a theology of the periphery. Therefore, it is a theology that will clearly propose critical points of support for Latin America but also for the Arab world, for Africa, India, China, and for the blacks and Chicanos of the United States. By far the greater part of humanity!

And as this majority turns against the center, this theology becomes valid for the center as well, because it points out to them the pathway of their own liberation, or, better still, of their conversion, their dispossession. The conversion of the center will not be affected by the hippie movement but only by total dedication to the poor. Those who aren't so dedicated will never be converted. In a way their Christianity will become more and more an embarrassment for them; they will not know what to do with it. It will continue to chide them. They will come to realize that alms are not enough but that justice is demanded of them. Do you remember the "aid to underdeveloped countries"? This was bank loans to the countries of the Third World at high interest rates. This is aid? It is now clear that there is no generosity in the center but, rather, systematic exploitation. When Christianity refuses to be critical of this sort of thing, it becomes ideologized, it begins to close in on itself and to believe in the poor no longer.

Latin America right now has a fantastic responsibility. If I am correct in saying that the Latin American church is, by a design of Providence, situated within the poverty of the world, not by choice but by birth, then we have a great deal to do in the world of the near future. If the Latin American church does not commit itself to liberation, worldwide Christianity will have nothing to say to Asia or Africa. If this is so, we should no longer talk of liberation theology or of Latin American theology, but of a theology of the world of today. Understand "world" to include the center and the periphery.

Revelation of the Interpretative Categories

Before asking what theology is, we should ask what revelation is and consequently what faith is.

First, what is revelation? I will give a general definition and then go on to explain it phrase by phrase. Revelation is the alterative, existential "speaking" of God that manifests the interpretative categories or guidelines of Christic reality. To reveal demands that there be an other, because I cannot reveal myself to myself. I do not say anything to myself, I only remember things. Whereas when the other confronts me in totality and speaks to me the word that reaches my listening ear, that word is revelation. Revelation, then, is the word of the other that tells something *new* that I would not know unless it were revealed to me.

The opposite of revelation is delation. And how do I

get the other to delate? I torture him. Through torture I can get the other to say what he would be unwilling to say. Revelation is the word of the other given freely. But listening is demanded of me because if the other reveals something to me and I do not listen, there can be no revelation.

The word "revelation" by itself embraces the whole of humanity's experience, the face-to-face, totality and otherness and all that I have been talking about so far. There is no point even in beginning if this is not understood.

Philosophy brings about a clarification of the categories of totality and otherness as making possible an anthropological revelation. By this I mean that another person, in freedom, reveals himself or herself to me. And only then can we arrive at divine revelation and say that, if there is a God, it is possible that he would reveal himself. And philosophy stops here.

Theology begins at the precise point where we say Yes, God has revealed himself and he has said *this*. This means then that revelation is a "speaking," not just *what* is said but the actual saying of it; it is the "saying" of the other who by his word makes his presence felt and gives an answer to what he has been asked because the answer is not known. Hence, "he who has ears to hear, let him hear" is about the anthropological structure of hearing and also about revelation.

Revelation is an "alternative" speaking on the part of God. God first creates. This is metaphysical otherness at its cosmological level, because when the other was alone he created the things we call the cosmos. In the totality of the cosmos the absolute Other reveals his *new* Word and that is revelation.

The first Word, *constitutive* revelation, is that "the Word was made flesh." The Incarnation is the whole of revelation and at the same time the *reality* of what is later said. I indicated that "revelation" is the "speaking" of the Other, but of the "Christic" reality. Note that "reality" is not the same as Word. Christ saves and is now the salvation of humanity; he is the reality. But we have to uncover that reality because it is covered, and in order to do so, the Word enlighteningly reveals that reality. Thus we have to distinguish between the Christic reality (Christic instead of supernatural, which is not the right word) and the *revelation* of that reality. Christ is *real, grace is real;* supernatural means something not natural. But what is natural? Is the natural that which is cosmic, before the Incarnation? This can't be correct. Furthermore, we frequently believe that grace or the Christic is at times accidental and we confuse this with the "over and above," with *unreal,* whereas the Christic is the fullness of reality.

The Christic reality is truly, effectively, and constitutively what the Word of God reveals. Is what God reveals then this or that historical fact? No, what is revealed are the guidelines or the interpretative categories of that reality. This means that God does not reveal this or that to be good but reveals the criteria that allow me to discover what is good. When Jesus is asked, Who is god? he responds with a parable, which is the explication of the categories in the manner of *masal* (Jewish didactic method): "A man was once on his way down from Jerusalem to Jericho and fell into the hands of brigands who threw him to the ground. Then a Levite came; a priest went by and, lastly, a Samaritan drew near. . . . " He does not say, "You are good." He says, "Do this and you will be . . . . " In this *masal,* he reveals the interpretative categories which, when applied to concrete cases, will uncover the reality. We can see then that revelation, rather than manifesting concrete content, reveals the light that allows me to illuminate the concrete content.

These are what I call categories, guidelines, or criteria; with them we can take the measure of any past, present, or future historical situation. It is a matter, then, of knowing how to put these into practice. If I put them into practice, I am a Christian. Knowing what they are is the function of the theologian.

God, through revelation, gives us guidelines that are like a lantern. With it we are able, in the night of history, to discover a table, a window, a bench. God does not reveal the table, window, or bench, or any concrete thing. What God reveals to us is the light that then enables us to discover the meaning of the table, window, or bench in that light. We have said, "By the light of faith." It comes down to knowing precisely what faith is and who has it. Revelation is the alternative speaking of God in an existential way, that is, day by day, every day. Let us take a look at how this question can be stated.

Faith as Interpretation

I live in a pre-Christian world. I interpret everything in a certain way. To interpret is to unveil the meaning of something. When I say "table," does it make any difference if I am talking about a table for firewood or a metal table to be sold? Yes, because the meaning is different. If I am going to use it as firewood, it has the meaning of fuel. But if I need it to put something on, I interpret it as a table. If I sell it, I discover its economic meaning. The table is the same but the meaning is different. "Interpret" is not the same as "understand"—to interpret is to discover the meaning. I am in my world and in it I discover the meaning of something. Revelation is to reveal interpretative categories. Suddenly now I receive notice from someone, an indication, a light that introduces me to my world as a *new* world.

If I am a pagan Greek, I say "table" and "wood." The minute I say "wood" I think of "tree" and relate it to the "goddess of life." The meaning is that of the eternal return of the same. But if I am Christian and I say "tree," I think immediately that it is a creature at my service. That is quite different. This means that because of the mere idea of creation all things have changed their *meaning*, they are at my service, even the sun. Whereas in the light of the Greek vision, I adore the sun because the sun is divine. Quite different! What I'm saying is that the *meaning* of things changes according to the light. Hence, I say that faith is a light that existentially "exercises" the revealed categories.

Faith, then, is a light, but a light that is carried by the Christian community, passed from hand to hand. If I learn these categories, it is not because someone told me: "This is a category." It is rather because I experienced existentially how someone in the Christian community made use of it and, thus, in the face of this or that event, I discovered this or that meaning. In the face of one reality, I discovered a certain meaning and in the face of another reality, another meaning. Daily I began to give it the meaning that the Christian was giving it, not theoretically but in practice. And thus I began acquiring faith and I began to interpret things as the Christian interpreted them. In doing so, I was using the revealed categories daily and in a practical way to interpret reality. I was using them existentially and not as the result of deep thought. There is a difference. If we were to ask the Christian: What category are you using? he or she might well answer: What is a category? The Christian had never heard of such a thing and yet could be a hero, prophet, saint.

All that I have been saying here about categories I have said as a theologian. But the Christian, the *good* Christian, makes use of them perfectly but un-self-consciously. The Christian knows concretely what sin is but cannot explain it with categories. By the word "sin," the Christian means to become totalized. But I use a category explicitly whereas the Christian lives it implicitly; the Christian has had experience of what it means to "be closed off in oneself" like a god and to deny God the Creator.

Faith is a daily interpreting or a using of the guidelines or categories or the light that God has revealed and with which we discover the meaning of the reality, of the Christic fact which is developing, unfolding in the history of the people—in everything, in the way we drive a car, keep a diary, knot a tie, or spit. In everything, even in this nonsense of spitting—a sick man could refrain from spitting in the street so as not to spread his germs around. He would thus be serving his neighbor; he would be performing an act of love.

This means that in the little everyday things of life, there are being put to use these guidelines that either totalize us as being all that matters or open us to the other.

From all this it can be seen that loving your neighbor is the whole law. To love your neighbor is by no means a secondary moral norm. We mean, of course, not loving "your neighbor as yourself" but "as I have loved you." This is the *new* commandment, the new kind of love that transcends totalization. To love "as I have loved you" is to lay down one's life. Here, indeed, is a guideline. Those persons are Christian who day by day see the other as meriting their service even to the point of laying down their life.

The Christian life is a daily putting into practice of certain categories that have been received from the Other (the other in this case being the God of revelation in the tradition of the church) through the summoning voice of the poor.

Theology as the "Analectic Pedagogy of Eschatological Liberation"

What, then, is theology? In the first place, theology is reflective thought about these categories. That is, theology turns to the same shining light and reflects on it as such. Thought, then, is a turning to the daily and revealed categories in the Christian community, not to exercise them in day-to-day living but to situate them as *object*—in the sense of something brought forth from a *theoretical* consideration. But we are talking about the kind of theory that emerges from the praxis of a people and knows, furthermore, that the praxis is infinitely more worthwhile than the *abstract* description that the theologian gives. Thus, to think theologically is to reflect on the Christian day-to-dayness.

How and why should this be done? To "reflect on" is a *critical* position, that is, a crisis has come about in the day-to-dayness. Why should people want to do this? Because in their daily existence they have seen that there is lacking a certain clarification. The resulting confusion has become intolerable, holding back the process of liberation. The *crisis* in the church calls for a clearing up of the situation. Thinking as a vocation does not come out of nowhere but as the result of a breakdown, a crisis in the acritical day-to-dayness of the church. Here is where the need for clarity in regard to these categories is born and the vocation to theology enters.

If Latin America can now produce a theology, it will be, I think, because here in Latin America we are living through the worldwide crisis of the church in a very privileged way. The Europeans of the center are undergoing a crisis much less severe than ours. Theirs is the crisis of European modernity whereas ours is the crisis of the entire world. In that sense, because we are on the periphery, we are concerned with the crisis of all the poor peoples of the world, whereas those in the center take on only the responsibility for the crisis in their own world and they have no plan for liberation, no "way out" of their situation. They will be unable to find a way out on their own; this must come from the poor.

The thinking that arises from crisis is as deep as the depth of the crisis. The crisis in Latin America is much deeper than in the center. Therefore our thinking will have to draw more deeply, will have to take soundings from the beginning of the church until now and throughout the whole world.

Theology is thought that deals with day-to-dayness, not only to seek its concrete meaning at the moment but also to ask itself about the categories themselves that shed light on this day-to-dayness. What are these categories? I have been making use of them from the beginning of these chapters. I explained the notion of totality—it is the *flesh,* in the sense of the *world.* Here I was describing a category. It is one of the first lights, or categories, that both the Old and the New Testaments as well as Jesus and the church use. We have to think of it as such—as an interpretative category.

When the interpretative category of Christian theology was "substance" (*ousia*), as it was for the Greeks and, then, "accident" (as quantity, quality, relationship, and the other categories of Aristotle), we began with something that was given as substantial, *underneath* (*sub-*) appearances as an essence; then we went on to that which was supported, borne by, that is, the relative accidents. These were all categories also. But they were categories seen from within the Greek *totality*. Whereas if I question that totality as such, I place all the Aristotelian categories in crisis. But at the same time there arose new categories that were foreign to Greek thought. The category of "substance" turns out to be totally insufficient in describing the human phenomenon, because here the essential aspect is not substance but relationship. It was Thomas who said that person, in the Trinity, is a "subsistent relationship."

The Greek interpretative categories responded to a pantheistic understanding of the world where all beings, all things emerge out of "nature," having a certain form, substance. According to the metaphysical view of creation, however, everything is understood as coming out of the free option of God to create. The cosmos itself has an ethical status because it is the work of absolute Liberty. The category of Otherness (the Other as free beyond Totality) is the beginning: "In the beginning God created . . . " (Gen. 1:1); "in the beginning (*en arje*) was the Word . . . " (John 1:1). In the origin was the Other, whether as creator, as redeemer, as the poor who cry out for justice or as Christ who liberates.

And thus, Totality and Otherness, domination and oppression, sin and liberation or service, the old order and the new order or the kingdom are the categories revealed by God, lived out by the believer, thought upon by the theologian.

This is to say that theological thought is aware of its own categories; it uses them not only existentially but also gives thought to them methodically. Theology has a *method* that is not scientific or demonstrative, not dialectical but strictly analectic. The scientific method draws its conclusions from axioms. Theology does not demonstrate from axioms but from the poor, from Christ, from God who is beyond the system. Theology cannot be dialectical ("to go through" diverse "horizons") because the dialectical method starts with Totality, with the *flesh* and can only show the foundation of the flesh, of the system, of Totality; it cannot explore further. The method of the prophets, of Jesus, of Christian theology and, therefore, of liberation theology is analectic. That is, it rests upon a Word (the *logos* of analectic) that invades from *beyond* (the meaning in Greek of *ano* or *ana*) the system, Totality, the flesh. From the act that arises from beyond the cosmos (the Liberty that creates), from beyond history (the call of Abraham and Moses), from beyond Israel (in the Incarnation of the Word), from beyond every system (the poor as the epiphany of God), Totality is overthrown and a new world is born: the kingdom already born among us in history, which will come to full flowering beyond the human order at the end of world history.

Therefore, we can finally define theology as the analectic pedagogy of historico-eschatological liberation. Theology is borne along by the theologian. Theologians place themselves in political and erotic history as pedagogues. This relationship with the Other is not like that of the man-woman relationship, but neither is it like that of brother-brother or master-servant. It is neither erotic nor political. In this situation, theologians carry on the gift of prophecy and add to it a self-aware clairvoyance. Theology is teaching, it establishes the teacher-disciple relationship. Jesus was the *rabbi* of Galilee, prophet and Jewish theologian, educated in the synagogue and in his home at Nazareth. Theology is a pedagogy.

Its prophetico-pedagogical method is analectic. Its five stages can be summed up in the following way. (1) It confronts the facts of a system and refers them to the system as Totality. (2) It discovers their meaning in the

Epistemological Status   177

given world. In the bourgeois world it discovers that everything is interpreted as merchandise and as a means of getting rich. From that horizon it can explain everything that happens in the world. The movement of being to the horizon is dialectical; the movement of the horizon toward being is demonstrative or scientific. (3) The theologian begins his or her proper task in the analectic phase by making a judgment on the totality of the system (political, erotic, or pedagogic) from the standpoint of the revealing Word of God (categories), historical measures and, concretely, the summons of the poor of the system under consideration. (4) When we question the system from the exteriority of the Word, we are able to consider the fact of subjugation in the system (sin) and (5) the possibility of the praxis of liberation, redemption, or salvation (analectic praxis inasmuch as it would go beyond the system toward a plan for liberation).

For its part, this fifth stage is directed at the same time to a historical project for liberation (the next temporal, political, economic, erotic order), which is sign and testimony of the plan for *total, eschatological* liberation—the Parousia and the kingdom finally come.

Theology, then, is strategic support for the liberation praxis of the Christian, since it clarifies on a radical level the concrete, historical, somewhat veiled options that Christian faith daily interprets.